WHISTLES, SMOKE & STEAM

*Our train journeys around the world and
a guide to adventurous rail travel.*

Text and Photographs by

Pete & Pat Arrigoni

WHISTLES, SMOKE & STEAM

ISBN 0-9701423-8-2

FIRST EDITION
5 4 3 2 1

Printed in Canada

Published by the Book Division
of
Route 66 Magazine
PO Box 66
Laughlin NV 89028
www.route66magazine.com

This engine, a C-18, was built in 1895 by Baldwin Locomotive Works of Philadelphia, Pennsylvania. It has been displayed in front of the Durango Chamber of Commerce in Colorado as part of a Denver and Rio Grande Western train display since 1950. Known as the D&RGW #315, the locomotive was restored by the Durango Railroad Historical Society between 2001-2007 for operation at summer rail festivals. (www.drhs315.org)

PART ONE
Trains Offering Public Transportation

FOREIGN TRAVEL

TABLE
OF
CONTENTS

PART TWO

*Train Excursions and Tourist Rides, plus Oslo, Norway's Airport Express;
Bergen, Norway's Floibanen Funicular Railway; and San Francisco's Cable Cars*

FOREIGN TRAVEL

THE UNITED STATES

The Durango and Silverton Narrow Gauge steams over the "High Line" through the San Juan Mountains of Colorado.

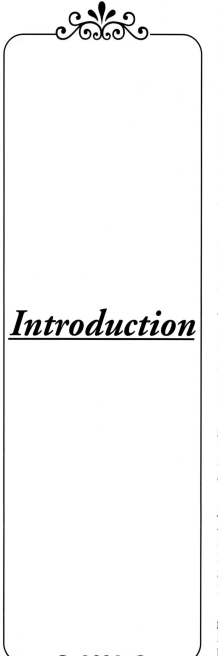

Introduction

When I was a child growing up in Illinois, there used to be a train that left Chicago and made the run south to Florida. I would hear its whistle as the cars raced along the edge of town and long to be riding in one of them.

One year I finally made it along with my mother. We rode south as far as Nashville, Tennessee where my sister was enrolled in a girls' boarding school. Now, at last, it was my turn. I was no longer a child standing on a hillside watching a train go by. I was now staring out the windows and seeing other kids waving and knowing they wished they were in my place.

When I married Peter Arrigoni, I soon discovered he was even more of a train buff than I. His father, who had immigrated from Lucca, Italy to San Francisco in 1923, used to take Pete and his brother, Bob, and other childhood friends to see the local trains. Pete also commuted on the famous San Francisco cable cars to attend high school at St. Ignatius. When we started traveling together, we selected itineraries which often included trains such as Amtrak in the United States, and dozens of train trips thoughout Europe, Great Britain, Scandinavia, South Africa, China and New Zealand. As a travel writer, I was sometimes invited to go on train trips with press groups to other locations, including Australia and Peru.

We also became interested in tourist trains, which are usually restored narrow-gauge railroads which were originally used for work purposes. These trains would haul logs out of Northern California forests or silver ore down the mountains of Colorado. The locomotives were powered by steam and many have been rebuilt and are operating all over the country.

Among the ones we have ridden are the Skunk Train in Northern California; The Durango and Silverton Narrow Gauge Railroad through the San Juan Mountains of Colorado; The Conway Scenic Railroad and the Mt. Washington Cog Railway in New Hampshire; the Cumbres and Toltec Scenic Railroad in New Mexico and Colorado; the Strasburg Railroad in Pennsylvania; the Cass Scenic Railroad in West Virginia; and the Grand Canyon Railway and the Verde Canyon Railroad in Arizona.

These railroad adventures have included riding on narrow, standard and broad-gauge tracks pulled by diesel and steam locomotives. Occasionally, we were allowed to ride in one of the locomotives and pull the train whistle at crossings. Great fun! Some trains across Europe and the United States had sleepers along with dining cars, bars and snack cars.

Join us as we relive our railroad adventures exploring Italy's Cinque Terra, and Japan by way of the Bullet Train. Ride with us on the *Midnight Sun Express* in Alaska, and Via Rail, one of the world's last extraordinary train-runs across Canada. Experience the historical tourist trains like the White Pass and Yukon Route Scenic Railroad, the El Transcantabrico in Northern Spain and the *William Tell Express* in Switzerland. Ride Amtrak from New York to Washington, DC and the Empire Builder from Chicago to Seattle.

All the trains written about in this book are still running and welcome passengers to ride them. Information for readers interested in taking these trains, including internet addresses, is provided at the end of each chapter. We hope readers will be inspired to duplicate some of these adventures.

NOTE: All times shown are in the twenty-four hour Universal Coordinated Time (UCT) adopted by most overseas countries. If you are not accustomed to this format, from midnight to ten, time is shown preceded by a "0", as in 0630 (6:30 AM) or 0930 (9:30 AM). From noon on, simply subtract twelve from the number. Thus, 1530 is 3:30 PM and 2130 is 9:30 PM.

The "*Canadian*" pulls out of Toronto for its 2775 mile run west to Vancouver.

Insert: Co-author Pat Arrigoni takes a ride in the cab of VIA RAIL locomotive #6402

CHAPTER ONE

THE *CANADIAN*
October 1992

PART 1

Trains Offering Public Transportion

The *"Canadian"* is ready in Toronto for the long trip west.

TORONTO, CANADA — VIA RAIL operates Canada's prestigious passenger trains and offers one of the last premier train rides in the world. Passengers riding in the beautifully restored, stainless steel cars of the *Canadian*, travel 2775 miles from Toronto to Vancouver. The route crosses Western Canada's vast prairies and magnificent Rocky Mountains, including the cities of Sudbury Junction, Winnipeg, Saskatoon, Edmonton, Jasper and Kamloops. Your travel agent can arrange side trips to Banff Springs, Lake Louise and Calgary.

VIA RAIL was created in 1978 by combining the Canadian Pacific and Canadian National Railroads. The *Canadian* provides Silver Class, Blue Class and Coach Class service.

Passengers departing Toronto at 12:45 p.m. on Tuesday will sleep on the train for three nights and arrive in Vancouver Friday morning at 8:00 a.m. The schedule is designed to allow people the opportunity to view Canada's gorgeous mountain scenery during daylight hours.

The train cars, restored in an art deco style, provide sleeping compartments, domed observation cars with lounges, an elegant dining car and a more casual Skyline Café. The sleeping car gives passengers a choice of bedrooms or roomettes. The bedrooms include an upper and lower bed, sink, 120V outlet plug, and a private toilet. Each sleeping car also provides one hot shower located at the end of the car.

When I made the trip from Toronto to Vancouver, what impressed me the most was the first-class equipment used by VIA RAIL. The staff was friendly and helpful and best of all, the food much tastier than I had expected.

I felt an air of excitement when the train pulled out of Toronto. Outside, the fall air was crisp and the trees were turning shades of burnt red and gold. From far away, the whistle blew two long, one short and one long blast, warning the world of our fast approach.

Soon I left the compartment and made my way to the Park Car, which contained an observation dome and two lounges where fellow passengers were drinking complimentary coffee and tea and enjoying the view.

For the next few days my world consisted of my compartment, the Park Car and Dining Car. In between, I made my way up and down the entire length of the train's twelve cars talking to passengers, the conductor, and other train personnel. I also kept a record of where we were by the mile posts alongside the tracks. A log book explaining the mile posts was provided by Via Rail.

The Dining Car offered three seatings for dinner, and two for breakfast and lunch. The dinner menu consisted of an excellent selection of fish, chicken and meats, along with soups, salads and desserts. Everything was properly prepared and delicious. The tables were covered with pink and white linen cloths, and there were fresh flowers, real glass dishes, and stainless steel utensils.

People played cards, read, or watched the scenery as the train sped along. We passed beaver dams, lumber mills, colorful aspen and birch trees, and groups of children waving at the passing train.

Then the lakes were gone and we arrived at the prairie. Growing in the fertile earth were crops of wheat, corn, barley, flax and soybeans. The train rushed on as hours and days disappeared. We rolled through the rugged Rocky Mountains past pine forests and snow-capped peaks.

The journey ended with a long run along the Fraser River, past the stretch of rapids called Hell's Gate.

And when we arrived in Vancouver it was with great memories of a magnificent train run across Western Canada.

On the Internet
Main site of VIA RAIL Canada:
www.viarail.ca/en_index.html
Route Guide:
www.viarail.ca/pdf/guides/en_canadian.pdf

Passengers enjoy the view from the domed observation car. Carolyn Nation of Hattiesburg, Mississippi on left.

CHAPTER TWO

LONDON TO PARIS
HEATHROW AIRPORT TO GARD DU NORD
June 2005

Gare du Nord, Paris.

LONDON — My husband and I, along with another couple, flew into London's Heathrow Airport from San Francisco. With our luggage in hand — two small bags each — we worked our way through a confusing maze to the London Underground, popularly known as "The Tube," where we caught a car on the Piccadilly Line to Piccadilly Circus. It was three weeks and two days before the London Underground bombings on July 7, 2005, but we were blissfully

unaware of what was about to happen. At Piccadilly Circus we transferred to the Baker Line and rode to the Waterloo Station where we boarded a Eurostar train for Paris.

It made my hair stand on end to read a few weeks later that Osman Hussain, a suspect in the

failed London Tube bombings on July 21, 2005 also boarded a train at Waterloo Station and slipped away, traveling from London through France to hide in his brother's home in Rome. He had also boarded a Eurostar train.

But getting back to our adventure, the car on the Piccadilly Line was clean with red and blue cushioned seats, gray speckled floors, blue metal poles and white ceilings. There was no graffiti, though the windows were badly scratched. Maps of the Underground ran along the insides of the car, near the ceiling, along with florescent lights and advertising cards. I found it difficult juggling two bags on the escalators and climbing up a couple of flights of stairs. It took around forty-five minutes to arrive at the Baker Line, and I noticed the people on the cars, crowded closely together, seemed careful not to make eye contact or chat with other passengers.

The cost of coming in from Heathrow Airport to Waterloo Station turned out to be just a little less than the four of us paid taking a cab on the way back. As there were many people coming in from the airport on the Underground with luggage it was crowded, forcing many passengers to stand.

When we arrived at Waterloo, we discovered there was a 4:06 p.m. train to Paris. We tried to move our 5:09 p.m. tickets up, but restrictions and costs were prohibitive. We sat at a bar instead and watched people rush around.

Small orange cards next to the ashtrays on the tables gave us pause:

POLICE WARNING

THIEVES ARE OPERATING NOW! WHO'S GOT YOUR PROPERTY?

They did not say anything about terrorists checking the place out.

Eurostar required that we check in at 4:30 for our 5:09 departure (17:09 UTC). We did go through a security check, though it was not as extensive as those at airports. We finally boarded and were in Coach One, Class Two. My seat was 24. Our coach was beautiful and clean and looked new. The seats were in groups of four with

Waterloo Station, London.

tiny tan plastic tables which could be folded up on each side to make them narrow. Small gray plastic wastebaskets were attached to the wall under the tables. Above each seat were individual reading lamps.

The upholstered seats were gray and brown striped with a matching tan-carpeted floor. The ceiling was gray. Above the seats were hard plastic luggage racks and a little lower, smaller racks with space for jackets or packages. There was also an area for luggage at the end of each car.

I talked with Mustapha, the Train Manager, who lived in Paris and declined to give me his last name or let me photograph him. Still, he was helpful and told me that the Eurostar is powered by a 25,000 volt electric line and travels on the same tracks as the French TGV trains. While the Eurostar runs at speeds as high as 186 MPH per hour *(300 km/h)*, the TGV trains can reach just over 200 MPH *(330 km/h),* though most run at 300 km/h top speed. In the

Chunnel Tunnel the Eurostar must slow to 100 miles per hour *(160 km/h)* because of wind problems.

Our train could carry 836 passengers in eighteen coaches with six designated first-class. Hot meals were served to those in first-class though there was no formal dining car on the train, only snack cars. The dinners for first-class passengers were provided by caterers from Brussels, Paris and London.

I learned from Mustapha that the crossing under the English Channel, between England and France via the Chunnel, would take approximately twenty minutes. This engineering marvel, built by England and France, was finished in 1990, then placed on the market for sale to private enterprise. It was the successful culmination of a centuries old dream to connect the United Kingdom to the European Continent. The first train ran through it in 1990 and the first commercial train in 1994. Its tenth anniversary of passenger service was celebrated in 2004.

Eurostar station, Paris.

"Passengers can take a train from Paris to Disneyland in France on Eurostar which takes about half-an-hour, or a direct train from London to Disneyland, a popular route," Mustapha informed me. "The Eurostar trains are also favorites with English visitors traveling to the South of France, or skiers going up to the Alps in winter."

The configuration of the train I was riding on was as follows: Coaches One through Five were second class and contained from 48 to 58 seats; Coach Six was a bar car; Coaches Seven - Twelve were first class with 25 to 39 seats; Coach Thirteen was the second bar car; Coaches Fourteen - Seventeen were second class and had 58 seats each, while Coach Eighteen was second class and contained 48 seats.

The restrooms were roomy, made from a hard plastic and painted gray and white. On some

you just pushed a button to open and close the doors. Water and air came down automatically in the sink to clean and dry your hands. Above the sink was a three-paneled mirror, and the toilet paper consisted of tiny sheets of pink paper.

As I walked through the cars, I noticed some seats were configured like those on an airplane in single rows with trays that lowered in front. I liked my second-class coach better. It seemed roomier with the four seats facing each other.

We rolled out of London past red brick and stucco houses. Graffiti was everywhere, but the sun was shining and the sky was blue with fluffy white clouds. Out the window I could see green fields dotted with bright orange poppies. We followed a major highway route off and on, crossed a river, and passed through several tunnels. The tracks were in good condition and smooth.

Past the tunnels but still in

England, we whizzed by red-roofed farm houses set in rolling hills among fields of sheep and lambs. I noticed that the soft rocking of the train had put many people to sleep. Few passengers seemed to notice the black-and-white dairy cattle lounging in the fields of white spring wildflowers. Most travelers were dozing, reading, working on laptops or chatting with friends.

The train came to a stop at Ashford International, a station which serves Southern England. Many jovial business men, on their way to Paris, boarded the train. The ride was still smooth as we passed more fields of sheep. At 6:00 PM we were again paralleling a divided highway with three lanes and a large toll station.

An announcement awoke everyone, telling us it was 7:10 PM and we were entering the Chunnel heading for France where the time was an hour ahead. We adjusted our watches as we raced under the

Aboard the Eurostar, London to Paris.

water of the English Channel toward the Continent of Europe. I had ridden a train through the Chunnel once before, but was still amazed we could arrive in France so quickly. When I had sailed across the English Channel on ships years back, the crossing took hours.

Now it took only twenty minutes to pass through the totally dark Chunnel before we found ourselves in the bright French countryside, which looked a lot like the English countryside. It was dotted with red-roofed farm buildings set among green rolling hills. The ride was still smooth though the train seemed to pick up speed and we felt more of a roll. There were rows of Italian cypress, stucco buildings set among yellow wildflowers, distant church steeples, crops of wheat, green fields of onions and Brussels sprouts. The

landscape was amazingly tidy. We zipped by more black-and-white dairy cattle, hay rolled in light plastic, two-lane country roads, and a greenhouse made of plastic.

At 8:00 PM it was totally light outside. By 9:10 PM it was still light, though beginning to dim as we arrived in Paris. Our Eurostar train had not stopped in Lille, France where we planned to board for our return trip to London and flight home.

As we pulled into Paris I counted fifteen or so tracks of railroad lines at Gare du Nord, a maze of overhead electric wires, and more graffiti. We were back in a heavily populated metropolis and headed into the heart of Paris, one of the most beautiful cities in the world.

Beginning in September 2005 Eurostar replaced First Class with separate business and leisure services. On the website they wrote, "It works like this: if you want to get there quickly and simply — choose Standard. If you want to travel in style, choose Leisure Select, and if you want to travel in style and get some work done, choose Business Premier."

Internet: www.eurostar.com

CHAPTER THREE

SEEING EUROPE IN COMFORT FROM ITS CRACK TRAINS
1982, 1983, 1985, 1986, 1987, 1988, 1990, 1992, 1998, 1999, 2000, 2002, 2007

High-speed Spanish AVE train runs between Madrid, Cordova, Seville and other stops.

The European rail system is a blessing for travelers. The trains are comfortable, fast, and punctual, while providing city-center to city-center service. Unlike air travel, when you arrive at your destination there is never a concern about how you will get into the city. Train passengers can immediately get tourist information, exchange currency, have a bite to eat, and hire a taxi.

Travelers from United States have known about the popular Eurail Pass for decades, and I have been fortunate to use it many times. Over the years individual countries have also offered their own passes such as the Rhine Countries Rail Pass, which includes Germany, Switzerland and the Netherlands; the France and Italy Pass; BritRail Pass or Eurail Selectpass.

One spring my husband and I toured Europe with a Eurail Pass and covered eight countries. On another occasion we explored five countries more extensively. We visited the cities of Frankfort, Paris, Lyon, Pisa, Geneva, Rome, Bologna, Venice, Milan and dozens more smaller towns and villages. We rode in the luxurious French TGV trains (the fastest trains in the world), the super fast TEE's (Trans-European Express), the elegant IC's (Inter-City), and a variety of local commuters.

The Eurail Pass works like this: You buy it before you arrive in Europe and it may be good for various amounts of consecutive-day travel, such as fifteen days, twenty-one days, one month, two months, or three months. Passes are good for unlimited first-class rail travel. A Eurail Youthpass for those under 26 is for unlimited second-class rail travel. You must have your Eurail Pass validated at a European train station before you take your first ride. From then on, just jump on any train, show your pass and you are home free.

There are a few exception to this "just jump on" advice. The

French TGV trains require a seat reservation. Reservations are also recommended for the TEE trains.

A Eurail Pass can take you to Austria, Belgium, Denmark, Finland, France, Germany, Greece, Holland, Hungary, Ireland, Italy, Luxembourg, Norway, Portugal, Spain, Sweden and Switzerland. There are over 100,000 miles of tracks from which to choose, plus many private railroads, buses, ferryboats and steamers, including those on the Rhine, Danube and Swiss Lakes. There are also ship crossings from Italy to Greece, Sweden to Finland, and Ireland to France.

A word of advice — pack light. On my last Eurail trip I took only a backpack, camera case, and purse. Luggage can get very heavy when you are dragging it up and down the stairs to the train tracks.

Some of my favorite European train rides have included a ride through the tulip fields of the Netherlands in spring, a run along the Mosel River in Germany when the hillsides were thick with grapes, and a day's journey through the Swiss Alps.

The following are excepts from notes I took on a trip in the spring:

March 21: On a train from Annecy, France to Geneva, Switzerland. Sunny and beautiful... green fields, snow-capped Alps. Spring is beginning to blossom.

Train from Geneva, Switzerland, to Lyon, France. This train is brand new...colorfully decorated in orange curtains and orange seats, blue carpeting and blue ceiling.

March 22: We have arrived in Italy through the Pierre Menue Tunnel. Sunny...little houses nestled up steep hills, wind whipping snow off the mountain-tops. An old fort guards the pass.

Train to Giverny from Paris.

In Chimonte, Italy, two-story stucco houses with iron grille balconies and laundry flapping in the breeze...vineyards climbing the hillsides, orchards of fruit trees, villages perched on mountainsides... crashing waterfalls when least expected, ancient stone cottages, a sea of red roofs on a modern city in a valley below...

Coming into Turino, Italy. The fields are plowed, streams full with the melted snow off the mountains, ruins of an ancient fortress...

Riding along the Mediterranean near Genoa, Italy. A vivid blue sea, heaving surf, palatial homes and apartments...palm trees, flowers, little boats, all colors...stone walls, potted plants, olive trees, Italian cypress...

The train seats are green velvet with elegant brocade and net luggage racks trimmed in gold. It looks like the old Orient Express.

March 23: The Cinque Terra, Italian Riviera...we are on the upper part of a double-decker train riding along the Mediterranean. It is like riding on a cushion of air. After we explored the ancient village of Vernazza, this train is like a modern fairytale. The seats are green, very soft. We are with friends and occupy four seats facing each other. There are glass windows that come up the side and over the top like glass Venetian blinds, and they can be opened.

The sea is a vast blue below us...we enter a dark tunnel, but there are openings so we may look down at the sparkling Mediterranean. We come out of the tunnel to a town terraced with houses on a cliff... whole villages sit perched on precipices that defy all building codes.

March 29: Leaving Rome for Bologna on the luxurious Italian train, the *Settebello*, which operates between Rome and Milan. (*Current service is called Eurostar Italia.*) Our car is blue and white. I decide on breakfast and am delighted to find a dining car with white tablecloths and red leather chairs. Breakfast is Continental and I am served juice, coffee and a sweet roll or biscuit.

Lunch, I learn from the menu, consists of antipasto, followed by pasta or rice, meat, chicken or fish, and a choice of cheese, a sweet, or fruit. The dinner menu is the same.

The AVE train in Cordova

After eating I decide to relax in the observation car, which is bullet-shaped with new swivel seats. The engineer sits in a compartment above us. We rush along the rails entering dark tunnels lit only by occasional neon lights.

April 3, Easter: We are on an IC (Inter-City) train called the Metropolitano, running from Milano, Italy to Dusseldorf, Germany. We will travel for eleven hours through Italy, Switzerland and Germany. Before boarding we purchased a picnic lunch at the station in Milano. For very little cost customers could pick either a veal or chicken lunch which included salami, three rolls, cheese, a small bottle of wine, a dessert and an apple.

There are three seats on each side of our private compartment. Each slides down and meets in the middle to form three single beds. The seats are an aqua color and there are orange curtains and brown carpeting. Heat pours from a wall unit under the window. The large double window has another narrow window at the top, but

nothing opens. There are two tiny pull-out tables, and two sets of gold-colored luggage racks.

At Chiasso (past Como) on the Swiss border, we used to have our passports checked, but no more. In Lugano, the lake is blue and beautiful…houses perched on the mountain sides…mists hanging on the mountaintops…occasional swimming pools at resorts along the lake…

We pass through a town called Paradiso, Switzerland, with a gorgeous view of the lake. How wonderful to live in Paradise! At Lago (Lake) de Lugano, I see occasional stone walls, modern apartment houses and trams running up mountain sides.

There are yellow wildflowers along the tracks. Sunny…snow on the mountaintops…a stream full of rocks creates white-capped rushing water. As we climb higher, it is greener…beautiful clean stream with a man fishing…an old stone church sits in a lush meadow. It snows as the train climbs toward the San Gotthard Tunnel.

A winter wonderland! We have

come out of the tunnel into a little ski village. There are pine trees heavy with snow like flocked Christmas trees…rugged rocks, many tunnels…sudden mountain streams or waterfalls that disappear as quickly as they appear…deep valleys…a village church with a tall steeple.

At Lake Luzern (Lucerne) Switzerland, steep mountains drop straight into the water and mist hangs over the lake as in a Japanese scroll. Mountaintops are lost in clouds and mists. I feel I am in another world, a fabulous place of endless tracks and comfortable trains that let me explore at my leisure without end for as long as I desire.

For up-to-date information on the Eurail Pass: www.raileurope.com

A Eurail Pass allows the boarding of a train, but does not guarantee a seat. Seat reservations are optional for most trains but are mandatory for all TGV, Thalys, Cisalpino. AVE and ES trains and selected EuroCity and InterCity trains and for all sleepers and couchettes. Couchettes: all tickets are sold which include any necessary reservations whether selecting a seat or sleeper. If holding a railpass, reservations are sold at passholder fares. Flexi Passes: The only difference between the Eurail Pass Flexi and the Eurail Pass lies in the duration of your travel. With the Flexipass, you may choose either ten or fifteen days of unlimited travel in seventeen countries within a two-month period.

Below, left: Jean Vaccaro of Fairfax, California rides an express train between Geneva, Switzerland and Lyon, France using an Eurail Pass.

CHAPTER FOUR

A FAST TRAIN FROM PARIS TO LYON
March - 1983

In 1981 a revolutionary train had its first trial run in France and the speed, comfort and service of this very spectacular train created a huge impact. Known popularly as the TGV or Trains a Grande Vitesse (trains of great speed), the train achieved speeds of up to 237 km/h (156 mph) with an average cruising time of 162 km/h (101 mph). The beginning trials from Paris to Lyon shortened the time for that run from three hours-and-thirty minutes to around two hours-and-thirty minutes.

TGV Trains in Paris station, Gare de Lyon.

Interior of TGV Train.

work and fluorescent lights with cross bars over long ceiling strips. Inside there was bustling activity, various stores, candy, coke and ticket machines, and continuous loud announcements. We finally discovered the room where we were to pick up our reservations for the next day's train. There were several lines, and above each line was a window with a clock telling when the line closed: 4:30; 5:00; 5:15, etc. You could stand in line for an hour and be out of luck when you finally got to a window.

The clerk who took care of us, after we had waited in line for 25 minutes, did not speak English, but we had put what we required in writing. The man turned to his computer and after what seemed an interminable time, gave us a card with four reservations.

Each TGV train is a single 660-foot-long unit with an engine at both ends. Eight passenger cars hold 111 persons in first class and 275 in second.

I rode this famous "bullet train" from Paris to Lyon one spring while traveling on a Eurail Pass with my husband and another couple. TGV trains leave from the Lyon Train Station in Paris (Gare de Lyon). When we went to pick up our seat reservations, which are required on all TGV trains, we were impressed by the classic beauty of the station from the outside. The interior had been remodeled, with low ceilings supporting grille

The next morning the TGV train, number 613, left Paris Gare de Lyon at 9:15 a.m. Our arrival was to be the Lyon Perrache Station, scheduled for two hours and forty-five minutes. The train, though packed on Friday night, was virtually empty Saturday morning. We found our car, climbed aboard, and sat down. The seats faced each other, with a gray folding table between them. Except for those particular seats, the rest all faced forward as in an airplane. There was an exciting whining of the engines as the train started up. People began running to make the last car, creating a high level of noise and commotion. I saw couples with tears kissing goodbye, and groups of people waving.

We started slowly and right on time, moving through the tremendous Paris train yard in the industrial part of the city. It was cloudy and overcast. I decided to explore and found that in first class there were two seats on one side and one on the other, while second class had two-by-two seating. I also learned that dinner was served to first-class passengers on carts similar to those on airlines. A bar car mid-train served snacks and drinks.

We left the Paris suburbs and were soon in the country. Fruit trees were blooming. Small villages would suddenly appear and just as quickly vanish behind us. We followed a river, then passed forests with stacks of firewood ready for winter. Ancient stone houses stood among plowed fields. At 9:55 a.m. the conductor checked our reservation cards and Eurail Passes.

In the refreshment car the menu posted behind the copper-topped counter advertised quiche, pizza, sandwiches, Perrier water,

TGV Trains in Paris.

orange juice, Pepsi, Kronenbourg or Heineken beer, martinis, whiskey, wine, cognac, coffee or chocolate. A service charge of 15% was added to everything.

By now we were rolling through small towns so quickly we could hardly read their signs. After Paris we passed through Laroche-Migennes, Montbard, Dijon (home of the famous mustard), Beaune, Chagny, Charlson-sur-Saone, Tournus, Macon, Villefrance-sur-Saone, and Lyon-Brotteaux.

Our final stop would be the Lyon-Perrache station. We discovered the printed schedule we had picked up in Paris showed us arriving there at 11:15 a.m., which was a mistake. Our Eurail guide timetable listed the correct time — 11:54 a.m.

The Gare de Perrache in Lyon is another sample of the old and the new. In front of a beautiful traditional European train station was an ultra-modern annex. On the ceiling was blue grille work hanging below orange and yellow bubbles forming beehives through which the sun shone in an array of colors. Escalators ran up and down in plastic tubes. The annex held shops, offices, snack bars, restau-

rants and a bus terminal — all noisy with foreign voices and urgent announcements.

Our super-fast TGV ride had been an exciting adventure on one of the world's fastest trains, and I look forward to riding it again.

These trains are now running 300km/h (187 mph) putting them on a par with the German ICE trains and the Japanese Shinkansen, making the trip between Paris and Lyon in two hours-and-two minutes. A double-decker train is new among the TGV's making the run from Paris to Lyon, and the trains now go to Marseilles. It is worth noting that Paris has six train stations and the all train times posted in these stations are based on the 24 hour clock.

For the latest information on Eurail Passes:
www.raileurope.com
Eurail also has a "France and Italy Pass"
which can be found on this site, as well as
single European country passes.

13

CHAPTER FIVE

EXPLORING ITALY'S CINQUE TERRA
1979, 1983, 1999

Train station in Vernazza, Italy.

Mention to a veteran traveler that you are planning to spend a week in the Cinque Terra, and you will most likely receive a blank stare. Explain further that this area is northwest of the Gulf of La Spezia on the Ligurian Sea and you might get some recognition. Finally, remark that this is the Riviera di Levante, known more popularly as the "Italian Riviera," just south of Portofino, and your listener will know exactly where you are going.

Cinque Terra, which translates to "Five Lands," boasts of a maritime population which predates Rome. The Ligures were fishing off these little ports in 200 B.C. The five towns nestled at the bottom of steep rugged coasts are still undis-

covered by most tourists. You can visit them by rail, water, a hiking trail or a tortuous road.

When I first explored some of this coast area by car, I found the roads so steep, narrow and curvy that I decided to park the car and take a train. Tiny coastal villages along the Ligurian Sea, which had taken hours to reach by car, were arrived at in minutes by train. The trains ran so frequently that I could get off in any village, stay as long as I wanted, then jump on the next one and keep going. There were many tunnels, but they all had openings so I could see the crashing sea below.

The region of the Cinque Terra extends from the northernmost town of Monterosso, south through the villages of Vernazza, Corniglia,

Manarola and Riomaggiore. Boats run from Genova to Monterosso and Vernazza, with several stops which include Portofino, Santa Margherita, Rapallo and Sestri Levante. You can also take a train south from Sestri Levante to the Cinque Terra.

The towns consist of pastel-colored houses three or four stories high, perched on the edge of the water and connected by long flights of steps and narrow dark alleys. Flowering gardens add a bright array of color above the sparkling blue sea. Terraced vineyards cover the rocky soil and stretch up out of the valleys, over the hilltops and into the next town. Often there are small inlets used by fishermen to haul in their boats. Occasional dark tunnels bring the sea water rushing right up under the villages.

In Vernazza we stopped in a bar for a cold beer and discovered an opening to the translucent blue sea water located below. It was inside a room where old men were playing cards. I found out later that there is a large deep grotto here called "The Devil's Den," which penetrates the underground of Vernazza.

Along the Cinque Terra there are magnificent views of the transparent aqua-colored sea, the immense horizons, the flowered terraces and the villages built in tiers down to the water.

MONTEROSSO AL MARE - This town has a sandy beach with sweeping views of the coast. To the

Vernazza, Italy.

north, one can see the Punta del Mesco, northernmost point of the Cinque Terra which contains the ruins of St. Anthony's Abbey. To the south one can view the towns of Vernazza, Corniglia and Manarola to the Punta di Montenero. Hotels have been developed at Monterosso al Mar in the hillside quarter of Fegina.

VERNAZZA - This gorgeous medieval village, built on a rock promontory, can boast of a 14th century church and an ancient fort. The parish church, built in 1318 on a rock three-fourths surrounded by the sea, is called Santa Maria d' Antiochia and its bells will delight you.

When one departs from the train, it is just a short walk down a narrow street where children play soccer to the town square at the edge of the sea. A safe harbor for boats has been created by partially diking off a small inlet.

Ambitious visitors can climb the long winding flight of steps to the fortress above for a breathtaking view of the Ligurian Sea and the village below. There is a small restaurant where you can stop for a drink on the way up. A tiny beach is located on the far side of the promontory away from the harbor.

CORNIGLIA - You will recognize the train station at Corniglia by the pots of colorful geraniums. Situated on a rock overlooking the sea, Corniglia is famous for the 1335 Church of St. Peter built on the ruins of an even older church. Its marble open-work rosette window, a work of Matteo and Pietro da Campiglio of Pistoia, is known world-wide. The mountain slopes surrounding the town are covered with vineyards which supply grapes to make the famous wines celebrated by 14th century Italian authors Boccaccio and Petrarch.

MANAROLA — The tiny ancient village of Manarola, with yet another 14th century church, is built on a rocky pedestal above the sea. Its tall, brightly-colored houses, which seem to lean against each other, are built in tiers leading down to the water. Terraces with bright flowers add to its charming atmosphere. A small creek running into the rock provides shelter for the fishing boats. It is here that the Via dell' Amore (Road of Love), a footpath carved out of the rock and overhanging the water, winds its way south to Riomaggiore. It is a romantic walk offering stunning views.

RIOMAGGIORE - Founded in the eighth century, the medieval village of Riomaggiore was made famous throughout Europe by Tuscan artist Telemaco Signorini. Located in a small valley surrounded by olive trees and vineyards, Riomaggiore lies at the mouth of a river which is today mostly covered over. The sea is reached by long flights of stairs where the beach is tiny and surrounded by rocks.

Fishermen may be seen here repairing nets and drying fish (sardelles) in the sun. The tall narrow houses of the village, connected by small bridges, steps and dark alleys, are often painted in pinks, red and blue with green wooden shutters.

Although Vernazza is my favorite spot in the Cinque Terra, any of the five picturesque villages with their towering cliffs, clear blue sea, olive groves and endless vineyards will astonish and delight you. I have found the route along the Cinque Terra to be one of the world's most dazzling train rides.

For up-to-date information:
www.cinqueterra.com

CHAPTER SIX

CELEBRATING RAIL TRAVEL IN THE NETHERLANDS
July 1989

Trains at Valkenburg.

In 1989 I was invited to the Netherlands to participate in a celebration of the 150th anniversary of the Dutch railroad. The Dutch call their train system a "public transport paradise" and with good reason. At that time on every working day, 4,300 passenger trains carried between 500,000 and 600,000 travelers. To Americans, especially those of us who rely almost solely on the automobile, the service seemed miraculous.

I found I could arrive at any train station in the Netherlands anytime between 5:00 a.m. and 1:00 a.m. (starting at 7:00 a.m. on Sundays and holidays) and in a very short amount of time catch a train to anywhere — usually within half an hour.

The main lines supplied even faster service. Four to eight trains ran every hour in both directions.

To celebrate the 150th anniversary of this fabulous service, the Dutch Railroads organized a huge summer exhibit in Utrecht. Visitors were invited to ride on a 1924 double-wagon train that provided a shuttle service to the Dutch Railroad Museum housed in the former Maliebaan Railway Station. This permanent collection had been remodeled and contained antique steam locomotives, carriages and trams.

Train buffs examined working model trains, old uniforms, badges, tickets, schedules, and a 1900 signal house that illustrated the way historic signaling systems worked.

To help celebrate the train jubilee, the Dutch Railroads added several one-day excursions to their program. These day passes combined a second-class round-trip train ride to the tourist attraction, local tram or bus fares if necessary, and the entry fee.

I decided it would be fun to do two excursions which included riding an old steam train from Hoorn (north of Amsterdam), and visiting the miniature town of Madurodam in the Dutch seaside resort of Scheveningen. I visited

Madurodam first and found that it faithfully reproduced Holland's most famous places on a small scale. I strolled by tiny ancient cathedrals, handsome railroad depots, monumental town halls, city streets and old canals. I actually felt like a child again playing in this make-believe doll-sized city.

In Amsterdam, there were replicas of the Anne Frank House, a shipping port, the Dutch Railroads, a sports park, an airport, the Peace Palace in The Hague, a beach with nude bathers, and bulb fields with colorful tulips.

At night the miniature city was lit with 50,000 tiny lights, turning Madurodam into a fairyland. Visitors sat in a grandstand listening to stories told in English, Dutch, German and French.

The town of Hoorn, where we caught a steam train for a "triangle excursion," was a picturesque village about a half-hour's train ride north of Amsterdam. Trains leave Amsterdam's Central Station for Hoorn every half hour. I arrived there a little before 10:00 a.m. and had over an hour to kill as the first steam train did not leave until 11:15 a.m. Fortunately, there was a well-stocked gift shop with toy trains, cards, posters, whistles, silver charms and other train-related paraphernalia. Just a short distance away was a museum of antique rolling stock.

The green-and-red steam engine that pulled our train, "number 30," had only four wheels and was built in Berlin in 1908. The conductor reported our speed that day to be between eighteen and twenty-four miles per hour, and added that the train carried 250 passengers. He also informed us that the train ran just between May

"The Eagle," an antique steam engine.

and September.

Our route took us north for about an hour's run to a town named Medemblik on the old Zuiderzee, a sea that had been partially filled in to create new land.

We disembarked at the station, took a few photos and started a four-block walk through town to a motorized boat. Medemblik was a charming village with brick streets, shade trees, an open market and outdoor stalls selling cookies, sandwiches and wooden shoes.

We found our boat just past the local yacht harbor. It was gleaming white and quite large, with two levels containing areas for dining and a small outdoor deck in

back. The boat left for Enkhuizen at 1:15 p.m., a trip of an hour-and-a-quarter which was the second leg of the triangle. We had lunch and enjoyed smooth sailing with nice sea breezes and lovely views all the way.

The third part of the triangle was a second-class train trip back to Hoorn (second-class meant plastic orange seats instead of upholstered orange seats). It turned out to be a terrific day excursion and most enlightening to learn about the fabulous Dutch railroad system.

For up-to-date information:

www.spoorwegmuseum.nl/en/index.html - Dutch Railway Museum website
www.railmusea.nl/en_index.php - excellent site for Rail Museums in the Netherlands.

For information on rail passes:
www.raileurope.com/us/index.htm

CHAPTER SEVEN

JAPAN BY WAY OF THE BULLET TRAIN
September 1985

Bullet Train,
Kyoto, Japan.

Interior of
Bullet Train.

When traffic jams were reaching monumental proportions on major highways in Japan, government leaders decided to try and help solve the problem with an ambitious expansion of their highly successful Shinkansen "Bullet Trains."

One program set up to help visitors move easily throughout the country was the Japan Rail Pass (JRP). Like the Eurail Pass, the Japan Rail Pass was only available for purchase outside the country. They were sold in "Green," valid in superior-class green cars and green cabins, and "Ordinary." Tickets for children ages 6 through 11 were sold at half price. Younger than

that, the passage was free as the child could sit on an adult's lap.

The Shinkansen passenger trains had three routes that left from Tokyo and Omiya, north of Tokyo. The Tokaido-Sanyo route went east, the Tohoku west, and the Joetsu Shinkansen northeast.

Each route operated two types of service. "Hikari" trains stopped only at principal stations connecting Tokyo and Hakata, the farthest point to the west. The "Kodama" trains served all stations.

Scheduled speeds on the fast trains were 99 km/h (62 mph), up to the maximum of 130 km/h (81 mph). Officials hoped to achieve even greater speeds, up to 161 km/h (100 mph), and tests recorded train runs of up to 321 km/h (200 mph) and faster.

The bullet trains are controlled by a general control center in Tokyo that monitors trains, rail cars, track maintenance, electric power and the position of all trains along the line. In the first twenty years of operation, the Shinkansen carried more than two billion passengers without a single injury.

The number of cars on the Shinkansen trains ran from 12 to 16 cars with up to 1,481 seats. Most of the new track was on concrete viaducts with tunnels and railway bridges. Hazards such as auto crossings and sharp curves were eliminated so the trains ran smoothly over jointless, welded rails.

I rode a blue and white Shinkansen Hikari from Tokyo to Kyoto. It had 16 cars including a buffet, dining car and five cars in front for unreserved seats. Two were reserved for non-smokers. The rest of the cars had reserved seats with two designated as the deluxe Green Cars.

We left at 9:17 a.m., stopped in Yokohama and Nagoya, and arrived in Kyoto at 12:11 p.m., which was less than three hours to travel 310.5 miles.

Our reserved car had three upholstered seats on one side and two on the other. Special features included reversible seats, overhead aluminum racks, net bags, small trays on the backs of the seats, aluminum hooks for coats, and overhead lights. Large clean windows gave us excellent views of the tops of buildings from our elevated tracks.

Shortly after we boarded, a girl in a blue uniform came through selling food. We were not familiar with the snacks she was selling, nor could we understand the continuous announcements coming over the loudspeakers.

We decided to head back to the dining car for some coffee and a roll. This car had plastic tables bolted to the floor with blue, orange and red plastic chairs. The waiter said there were no muffins, toast or croissants, so I ended up with white bread and a slab of frozen butter.

The menu on the table was written in Japanese and English and included some Western dishes such as halibut, roasted chicken and hamburgers. The adjoining buffet had a counter but no seats. Passengers could check the train speed on the speedometer in this car (which indicated we were traveling 124 km/h [77 mph]), or make a telephone call to major cities along the line.

We passed Yokohama and found the landscape highly industrial. The train swayed heavily. A half-hour later we finally saw some farm country, and at 10:45 we crossed a river. Around 11:00 we saw green houses and a few rice fields. By 11:30 the country was getting more mountainous and prettier, though still highly developed.

The main problem I found with the Japanese trains was that there seemed little consideration for luggage. I did not see any porters, and as passengers we had to climb many steps at the stations lugging heavy suitcases and bags. There was no luggage storage compartment, so we had to push our suitcases into the small gaps between back-to-back seats.

Still, the equipment on the trains was all first class, the ride smooth; we got there fast and I enjoyed the experience tremendously. The Shinkansen services have expanded and the trains are now running up to 300km/h (188 mph) putting them on a par with the French TGV and German ICE trains.

For additional information:
www.japanrail.com
This is a good site maintained by the Japan Rail Group office in New York City.

There are two types of Japan Rail Passes: Green (for superior-class Green Cars) and Ordinary. Each of these types is available as a 7-day, 14-day, or 21-day Pass.
You must buy an Exchange Order from an authorized sales office or agency before you come to Japan.
After arriving in Japan, you turn in the Exchange Order to receive your Japan Rail Pass at an applicable JR station that has a JRP exchange office. You cannot buy the JRP inside Japan.
www.Japanrailpass.net

Japan Rail Pass website:
http://www.fact-index.com/s/sh/shinkansen.html

Restaurant cars were discontinued in March 2000, but there are now at-seat trolley services selling box lunches, snacks and drinks.

CHAPTER EIGHT

SWITCHBACKING TO PERU'S LOST CITY
May 2003

Train to Machu Picchu.

The fabled Inca city of Machu Picchu sprawls in the valley before me. It appears to be a magical place one might imagine in a dream. The rain and mist have given way to glorious sunshine and the day stretches before me as a grand adventure.

We are high up in the Andean Mountains of Peru, visiting one of the most famous wonders of the world. It is a lost city hidden so high in the mountains the Spanish conquistadors never found it when they conquered and plundered this country in the 16th century.

When Hiram Bingham, a Yale professor of anthropology, discovered Machu Picchu in 1911, the ancient ruins were known only to locals. He soon announced his findings to the world. Years later, in 1948, he inaugurated a switchback road built to the site. Today, visitors arrive by narrow-gauge diesel trains from Cuzco, then change to a bus for the ride up Bingham's road to the fabled city.

The train is operated by the Orient Express Company and leaves Cuzco at 6:00 in the morning. Our car, painted a shiny blue with yellow trim, provides comfortable seats with service trays and large windows. We are in the Vistadome, but there is also a less expensive Backpacker Service.

The train ride takes four hours to travel the sixty miles from Cuzco to Aguas Calientes where we connect with a bus to go up to the Inca city. We stop twice for people who want to hike the Inca Trail. We learn that there are four-days, three-days, two-days and single-day hikes.

The train trip begins with two switchbacks known appropriately as the "zig zag" out of Cuzco. We are in car one, the lead, with the engineer on the right side in front. We settle in as a light rain begins to fall. Soft guitar music plays from hidden speakers as we look out over a sea of red tile roofs in the hilly city of Cuzco. Our guide informs us that the city has a population of 400,000, extending to over a million if the environs are included.

We leave the heart of the city and travel through the outskirts. The houses here are built of mud bricks mixed with straw. Most have tin roofs held down by rocks. We see TV antennas, laundry drying, and small clay bull figurines perched on roofs. These *pucapucara* bulls, named for the city in which they are made in the south of Peru, are given to friends who have just moved into a new house. They are thought to bring strength and good fortune.

The sun is coming up behind the Andes as we roll into the countryside. We pass through small villages where people still dress in clothing influenced by the Spanish occupation. The women look more traditional in their full bright skirts and blouses. Many have a shawl wrapped around them, a *manta*, in which they carry a baby or small child. Often a tiny leg or foot will be hanging out.

By 6:30 we are up to 12,000 feet. We pass fields of corn, furry pigs and cattle. In the distance are the stunning snow-capped peaks.

Our first stop is Poroy, where the most ambitious hikers get off with their heavy backpacks. At 7:15 we are served tea and coffee, sandwiches of ham and cheese, a slice of pound cake and mixed fruit in a small cup. Our piped-in guitar music changes to a soothing piano recording. We notice rows of eucalyptus trees planted beside the tracks and the rushing Pomatales River below.

This river runs from the south to the north through the Pomatales Canyon and is the Sacred River of the Incas. They call it Urubamba, also the name of a town.

We begin to see the remains of Inca farming terraces and then the train ride ends at Aguas Calientes. We walk about fifteen minutes to where we will board the bus. The walk goes past dozens of souvenir

The Pomatales River, Peru.

stands, but we delay our shopping for the trip back.

When we finally arrive at Machu Picchu, we purchase our entry tickets and find we can check extra things we don't want to carry all day. The Sanctuary Lodge built at the entrance of Machu Picchu National Park will provide us with a delicious hot buffet lunch later in the afternoon.

While we have seen a few Inca ruins coming up on the bus, our first full view of the city brings everyone to a stop as they stare in wonder at the magnificence of this ancient site.

We begin our hiking tour, visiting highlights such as the mysterious white granite ruins of the Temple of the Moon, the Sacred Square, the Site of Three Doors, Temple of the Condor, the Row of Houses, Palace of the Princess, Temple of the Sun, the Sacristy,

Palace of Three Windows and the Main Temple.

We hike for three hours up and down granite stairs, also visiting the Industrial Region, the Quarry, and the Watchman's House, which sits high on a peak and has a spectacular view of the entire city. The Agricultural Area features the familiar Inca terraces seen extensively throughout the Andes.

I am amazed at the stunning beauty of this lost city. Hidden in mists below snow-capped mountains and vertical cliffs, Machu Piccu once offered its people a true sanctuary. One feels a profound peace in this high setting away from the crowded cities, above the roaring rivers and beyond the encroaching jungle. This protected citadel is breathtaking in its elegance, a magical place to be preserved for all time.

PeruRail provides transportation between Cuzco and Machu Picchu by Vistadome or Backpacker Service. The train leaves at 0600 and returns to Cuzco at 2020.
For up-to-date information:
www.perurail.com
In Cuzco call: 011-51-84 238 722
Ext 318, 319

Orient Express is now offering a deluxe train called the "Hiram Bingham" from Cuzco to Machu Picchu. They have added two dining cars, a bar car and kitchen car, and can carry up to 84 passengers. This train departs Cuzco at 0900 and arrives at Machu Picchu at 1230. The return trip departure is at 1830 and features cocktails, entertainment and a four course dinner. The train arrives back in Cuzco at 2200. PeruRail also has an extended train called the "Andean Explorer" that operates between Cuzco, Lake Titicaca and Southern Peru.

THE UNITED STATES
<u>CHAPTER</u> <u>NINE</u>

COMING HOME ON AMTRAK
Colorado to California
April 1979

Sparks, Nevada.

My fifteen year old son, Bob, along with his buddy and me, had been vacationing in Vail, Colorado. Rather than fly home to California, we decided to ride Amtrak. We boarded the *San Francisco Zephyr* in Denver for the 28-hour trip back to Oakland, California. I reserved a bedroom with two bunks and a private bath for the boys, and a roomette for me.

Before boarding we load an ice chest with Cokes, 7-Up, bread and crackers, six packages of sandwich meats, mayonnaise, mustard, pickles, olives, assorted nuts, potato chips, corn chips, beef jerky, cupcakes, a variety of juices, and a bottle of white wine for me. This should suffice between meals.

The boys settle in and begin to eat. I crawl into my compact roomette. It is decorated in purple: purple cushioned chair, purple carpet, and purple top of the commode, which is their polite way of saying toilet.

Facing the chair is an aluminum rack for luggage. Below is a mirror and a sink which folds into the wall. Other features include a 110 volt outlet, a shoe locker, and a tiny closet where a few items may be hung. The temperature is controlled by knobs on a panel for floor heat, air conditioning and a fan. I try the air conditioning but it does not work, so I switch on the fan.

Above the sink there are paper cups and a little faucet labeled "ice water." I push it and enjoy a cool drink. The feeling is a little like exploring a doll house.

At 1249 we are still sitting in Denver although departure time is scheduled for 1230. Finally we start, go for ten feet, and stop. For heaven's sake, I am riding backwards. They have put another engine on the back end of the train, and are taking it out the same way it arrived. Finally we begin again. People wave from the platform. Then we pick up speed and begin to sway back and forth, a sensation that will last for the next 28 hours.

We pass warehouses and a huge

railroad yard. I read the name of Burlington Northern Line, Santa Fe, Fruit Growers Express and others from all over the country. In the distance I watch the skyscrapers of Denver quickly recede as we hurtle along the tracks backwards.

The landscape is flat farmland, very dry looking, and dotted with white farm houses. Lines of laundry flap in the breeze. Old cars and deserted farm machinery fill the horizon.

At 1335 we slow down going through the town of La Salle and pass a tall water tower. The land looks like Texas during a drought. Everything is absolutely barren as we near Wyoming, not a tree or bush, just long flat lands with occasional hills.

I go to check on the boys. They are still happily eating and drinking. I return to my compartment and relax with a book, some corn chips, beef jerky, cashews and a cold drink. This is becoming fun.

Around 1500, one hour overdue, we arrive in Cheyenne. My son comes to fetch me. "Let's go outside and get some fresh air," he says. "The porter told me we have twenty minutes."

We climb off the train, legs wobbly, and walk through the old gray stone station and out the front door. The dusty town looks like something right out of a western movie. The boys stare down the street. My son's friend laughs and remarks, "The horses and cowboys should be galloping around the corner at any minute!"

"That must be the courthouse," Bob says, pointing down the wide western street to an impressive looking building at the end. I believe he is right.

Buildings, mostly brown,

Snow in the Sierras, west of Truckee.

except for one painted a bright red, stand three to five stories high. No skyscrapers crowd our view of this sleepy western town on this hot Saturday afternoon.

We hear the train whistle. "We'd better go," I urge nervously. "Daddy will never understand if we get stranded in Cheyenne!"

We return reluctantly to our stuffy compartments. The train starts, and I discover that I am riding forward. A new engine has now been attached to the front of the train. Terrific!

We roll through an imposing railroad yard, and past highways with billboards. By 1600 we begin to climb into foothills. I see pine trees and patches of snow along the tracks. The earth is a pinkish red. As we continue up, the desert-like landscape is dotted with large sculptured rock formations and stark buttes silhouetted against the late afternoon sun.

We pass rocky outcroppings, small ponds, then sudden sweeping vistas overlooking the plains. Unexpectedly, we enter a long dark

tunnel and come out on the flat empty prairie. Off in the distance stands a deserted windmill, beyond are the snow covered mountains. There is nothing else, not even a single ranch house. We are isolated, and I am reminded that this land appears the same now as it must have looked to immigrants who traveled west on the train a hundred years ago.

The next stop is Laramie. The brown-and-white frame station is bordered by a small park with dry grass and leafless trees. It is only 1630 but the street lights have been turned on.

The first call for dinner comes at 1715. The sky is now gray as the sun begins to set. We pass miles of snow fences built to protect the tracks.

Knock. Knock.

"Come on, Mom, we're starved!"

At 1800 we enter the dining car where the tables are set with white tablecloths and a single carnation in a bud vase. A waiter appears.

Martinez, California.

"Where are we exactly?" I ask.

He shakes his head. "I don't know. I never look out. I'm on this train six days at a time to Chicago and back, and I can't wait to get home to San Francisco!"

The menu is bright blue cardboard decorated with cartoons of a train, a smiling half-moon, and three cars filled with happy people. On the back is a beverage list with wine, beer, mixed drinks, plus soft drinks.

The entrees include burgers, chef's salad, hot turkey sandwich, New York steak, roast prime rib-o-beef, and pan-sauted trout. These selections come with a variety of potatoes, salad, vegetables, corn fritters and spiced apple rings. Children may eat one-quarter of a chicken or a chopped steak. Not my children. They could finish the entire chicken in thirty seconds flat.

I decide on the steak, and the boys order the burgers with cheese.

While we wait, Bob suddenly cries out, "Look! A herd of antelope! Over there!"

We stare out the window in fascination as fleeting antelope race across the flat Wyoming plain. What excitement! The animals move like the wind with a graceful gallop that soon has them gone from our view.

Our dinner is best forgotten. My steak is tough and chewy, although the couple of mushrooms on top taste good. The meat in the boys' cheeseburgers arrives paper-thin and charcoal black.

We skip dessert and walk back to the observation car where we stay until the sun sets. Here Bob meets an attractive young lady from Elko, Nevada. Through the darkening skies, wild ducks wing their way to quiet ponds, and romance blossoms in the observation car.

I crawl into my tiny shaking roomette around 2200. My bunk stretches from the purple cushioned chair up and over the purple covered commode, which means there is no possible way I could use this contraption if I needed it during the night.

The boys, still in the observation car, will not budge. During the night we pass through Ogden, Utah where we lose an hour returning to Pacific Standard Time; Elko, Nevada, where Bob's new girlfriend departs; Carlin and Winnemucca.

By 0800 we are coming into Sparks, Nevada. We have picked up some time crossing Wyoming and are now back on schedule. The weather outside is sunny as we parallel the swollen Truckee River. Along the river are migrating birds and people fishing, while off in the distance we can see snow-covered mountains.

The Sparks station is a two-story yellow frame building with an overhanging green roof and a large square observation tower. Our stop is brief as we are due into Reno at 0850. We pass the MGM Hotel, and I see advertisements for other big gambling casinos. An old man is sitting by the tracks with a sleeping bag under his arm eyeing the train with speculation.

We stop and an astonishing mob of people appears outside my window hurrying to board. Though some are carrying skis, most have come to Reno to gamble for the weekend and are now returning to the Bay Area. Four cars are added to the train and 350 more passengers climb aboard. They begin celebrating immediately.

We finally leave Reno, passing the El Dorado, Circus Circus, and Harold's Club. When we begin to climb into the Sierras, the air becomes cool and crisp. We pass pine trees, snow patches and waterfalls.

I make my way along the crowded aisles, through the packed dining car and lounges, to the observation car where I find the boys.

"We already ate breakfast, Mom. It was pretty good," Bob says.

"What did you have?"

My son smiles brightly. "Orange juice, two eggs, sausage, a side of ham, three English muffins, and two glasses of milk."

"I had pancakes, bacon, juice, eggs and toast," his friend informs me.

I peep inside the dining car. It is mobbed, so I return to the boy's bedroom where I make myself a bologna sandwich and a glass of juice.

The train continues to climb, and it begins to sleet, then snow. It is cold but invigorating to be crawling through deep drifts and the scene reminds me of one of those round, glass ball paperweights filled with thick whirling particles of "snow."

I leave my compartment to shoot a couple of photographs through the open window of the end platform. The train lurches to the right, and I am slammed against the side of the corridor. Three revelers who have boarded in Reno rush past me toward the lounge. I stagger to the door and push through to the platform which connects to the next car. I unlock one of the dirty windows and hook it open. Billows of snowflakes swirl past my face which suddenly feels cold, then wet.

Outside, the world looks like a Christmas card, even though it is April. Thick snow flurries land on ten-foot drifts along the track. In the distance the sleek silver cars of the train curve along the rails and rush toward a tunnel. The whistle blows a lonely distant cry.

Then in an instant we plunge into the darkness of the tunnel where the blackness is broken only once by a single dim bulb. I feel the sideways vibrations suddenly begin to slow. We emerge out into a brilliant snowy whiteness and come to a stop. What is the problem? Will we be snowed in? Will the high Sierras claim still more victims? People come into the platform area to stare out and make nervous jokes about the Donner Party. Nothing moves for about half-an-hour.

After what seems like an eternity, the train starts up again, s-l-o-w-l-y, but at least it is moving. I sigh with relief and make my way back to my single compartment.

At 1230 we are called to lunch. The train is moving down and out of the heavy snow although there are still some patches along the tracks. People are again lined up for food which features a "Late Riser Breakfast, chef's salad, chili a la San Francisco Zephyr," along with assorted sandwiches. Bob and his friend combine a beefsteak with chili.

"Our cooler is completely empty!" my son complains.

When we arrive in Sacramento, the capital of California, it is raining hard. At 1415 we are in Davis, a city located in an area of rich farmland and orchards. Then around 1500 we cross Suisun Bay on a high railroad bridge coming into Martinez. The rain has stopped, though it remains overcast and cool. We roll by multiple oil refineries and tank cars. Two small boys, lunch buckets in hand, stand on a hill pressed against a fence watching us pass with longing in their eyes.

The porter enters to see if I need any luggage tagged. "We'll be coming into Oakland soon," he informs me. I nod and watch out the window. First there is Richmond and the BART (Bay Area Rapid Transit) Station where hundreds of commuter cars are parked. Suddenly the sun appears, and it looks like a beautiful day in the Bay Area. Clouds are fluffy and white while the air through the open window smells truly fresh.

From Richmond through Berkeley to Oakland, we pass dump yards and warehouses. People inside the cars crowd the exits, joking and laughing, eager to be gone. Luggage is piled high, and it is worth your life to step out into the packed swaying aisles.

Oakland appears at last a little after 1600. My husband, standing in front of the impressive gray stone station, waves a cheery greeting as we all pile off. The luggage is claimed in short order and loaded into our station wagon. As we start off for home, I call "Goodbye!" to all the friends we have made on Amtrak.

"Hey Dad! You should have seen Mom trying to ski! She fell all the way down Copper Mountain!"

"Shut up, Kid!"

For the latest up-to-date information: www.amtrak.com

The California Zephyr now runs between Chicago and Emeryville, CA. and the train follows a more scenic route from Denver to Salt Lake City. Amtrak has upgraded the equipment over the past twenty years to Superliner rail cars.

CHAPTER TEN

AMTRAK'S "EMPIRE BUILDER"
CHICAGO TO SEATTLE
June 1984

AMTRAK steward, Michael Stallworth, at East Glacier National Park, Montana.

My husband and I decided to ride the famous *"Empire Builder"* from Chicago to Seattle with a stop at Glacier National Park, Montana early one spring. Amtrak allows unlimited stop-offs for no extra charge. Our route would take us from Chicago to Milwaukee, across Wisconsin to Minneapolis-St. Paul, across North Dakota and Montana, over the Rockies and the Cascade Mountains, to Puget Sound and finally Seattle. We would cover 2,281 miles, and spend three days and two nights on the train in a private sleeping compartment.

We arrived at the old Union Station in Chicago only to find that Amtrak uses a small, low-ceiling annex station across the street. As soon as we entered we saw signs posted everywhere warning us to watch purses and wallets.

We decided to put our bags in a locker, but there were more people needing lockers than were available. We finally found two tiny ones and as we were free of encumbrances until train time, were able to go to lunch.

At the departure hour we found ourselves in the lower level of the station and part of a huge mob scene of restless passengers waiting for two late trains, the *California Zephyr* and the *Empire Builder*. Employees of Amtrak dressed in white shirts, red vests, and blue pants or skirts, tried to keep order pushing everyone back behind velvet ropes. There was no place to sit down and no air circulation. We got hotter and hotter as the minutes passed.

There are five train sets that make up the Chicago-Seattle run. When a train arrives in Chicago

around 1500, it is cleaned and prepared for departure the next day at 1445. There seemed no good reason for this one to be late, but I found this was very common.

We had been waiting to board since 1400. Finally at 1500 the first 25 passengers were allowed aboard. We found our Deluxe Suite A in the next-to-the-last car on the upper story. I was delighted. It was certainly larger than any suite I had ever had on a train before, and appeared new and sparkling clean.

The wide seat, which faced forward, was upholstered in orange and tan. This made into a bed along with an upper bunk. The floor and ceiling were upholstered with a tan carpet.

The glass door to our compartment was covered with an orange curtain which could be opened to look across the aisle and out the

Forty-foot Douglas
fir trees in
Glacier Park Lodge.

window on the other side of the car.

Other features included a third chair which rode backwards, a folding plastic table, a sink with a three-way mirror, supplies of towels, washrags, Kleenex, soap, a tiny closet with three hangers, a private toilet, and a shower in the same compartment. This was managed by pulling a shower curtain in front of the bathroom door and by a clear piece of plastic which covered the toilet paper. There were two buttons to push: one flushed the toilet and one turned on the shower, and you had to be very careful to push the right one.

The compartment was air-conditioned, plus it had piped-in music (*which did not work*), a button to call the porter, and a loudspeaker for public announcements. There was no way to lock the door

from the outside if you wanted to leave for a while.

A conductor dressed in blue pants and shirt pounded on our door and asked, "Got your tickets?"

I produced our documents, and he was gone in a flash.

We pulled shakily out of Chicago past old brick tenements and warehouses, and followed the Chicago River. An announcement over the loudspeaker welcomed us to AMTRAK.

After a while I took a walk through three coach cars and a lounge car to the dining car to check on dinner. The coach seats, which were very roomy with a fold-up table in front of each one, all faced forward.

The lounge car had seats bolted to the floor facing the windows. The windows curved on the edge of the car, but did not extend

across the top.

The tracks were very rough, and I had trouble walking. We met our steward who had a colorful personality and was most helpful. He gave us a souvenir dining car menu and a train schedule, plus two small baskets with bottles of wine, bread, crackers, cheese and nuts.

We were due into Milwaukee at 1609, but were running 45 minutes late. We passed cornfields and small towns, a couple of lakes and freshly-planted fields of soybeans just sprouting. White houses with tall TV antennas dotted the landscape along with grain silos, dairy cows, and freight trains. The rails remained rough, and the telephone poles looked short from our second-story perch.

At 1650 we arrived in Milwaukee past junkyards of abandoned cars, a cemetery, a small residential area of wooden houses, and several industrial areas. The train passed over a river and went by a large, round-domed building and a church with gold crosses.

Milwaukee was a city of bricks… red bricks, painted white bricks, yellow bricks and black bricks covered with ivy. Old railroad tracks below us were covered with weeds.

Our service steward arrived and took our reservations for a 1915 dinner seating and gave us a white slip that said: "Admit one. Please be prompt." He informed us that the cocktail lounge was downstairs from the observation car, and they were now selling cordials.

Our route northwest out of Milwaukee took us to Columbus, Portage, Wisconsin Dells, Tomah, and La Crosse, where we crossed the Mississippi River into Minnesota.

I found Wisconsin very green and more rolling than Illinois. At 1715 we crossed a large lake with a sandy beach and wooded island. There were speedboats racing around and kids fishing off a pier.

Past the lake were fields of waving oats as lush as velvet and beyond, blue heron and wild ducks. To our huge enjoyment, a white-tailed deer came racing across a field.

We reached Portage, Wisconsin, at 1830 and saw that the fields of corn had been washed out by heavy rain. The Fox and Wisconsin Rivers were next, the Wisconsin Dells at 1853 hrs, a resort town with a red sandstone canyon and river that is a popular boating and rafting spot. The water here was swirling and muddy.

It was time to go to dinner. I followed a man and his wife through the coach cars. He said, "I have worked for the railroad for 25 years and have never been on such a rough line."

He looked ahead at his heavy wife. "I hope she doesn't fall down. I could never get her up again!"

I asked him if it was because we were on the second level.

"No," he replied. "It is because the tracks are not firm."

Dinner was a disaster. My husband's chicken and my salmon were both reheated and badly dried out. My lettuce with two tomato slices came in a plastic dish with the lip of two sides broken off. The dressing came in medicine cups. Everything was served on or in plastic. The tablecloth was paper.

Our service was worse. We could not get water, tea, milk or ice cream for the child across the table from us, or the cake and coffee we had ordered. When we finally gave up and were ready to leave, our waiter dumped a Coke all over the table.

We crossed the Mississippi River at La Crosse, which was high with flood waters. Houses along the banks had also been badly flooded. A pale sunset over the water gave it a magic quality and reminded one of Huck Finn and the old river boats. We enjoyed this for nearly an hour before retiring for the night.

Since I am a lot smaller than my husband, I volunteered to take the upper bunk. When finally made up, his was 26 inches wide, while mine was 15 1/2 inches. The upper bunk had a pouch connected to the wall for things like Kleenex and glasses, and a reading light, but they, along with the ladder, were at the foot end instead of the head

end. Now this certainly did beat sitting or sleeping in a coach chair all night, but I had to remember not to sit up. Naturally, I forgot once and smashed my head.

We slept through most of Minnesota and half of North Dakota, but woke in time to see some pheasant in the Devils Lake/Rugby area.

My breakfast of three pancakes, orange juice and coffee was much better than dinner. I was seated next to a man who was Vice-General Chairman for the Brotherhood of Railway Carmen for the Burlington Northern. He told me that AMTRAK passenger miles were up nine percent since the year before.

After breakfast I sat in the observation car while our room was being made up and watched the rolling green prairie glide by under a wide blue sky.

Since my husband had skipped breakfast, I brought him a cup of coffee from the lounge car downstairs. The lounge had three tables which could seat four people each, and eleven seats in a semi-circle facing away from the windows. At one end of the car was a stainless steel counter where a man sold snacks and drinks.

Our day passed pleasantly. We saw Fort Buford where Chief Sitting Bull surrendered after the Battle of the Little Big Horn, Fort Union, where we crossed into the Mountain Time Zone, and Wolf Point, Montana, so named for the wolf trapping and trading that used to go on.

From a National Geographic map I had brought along, I learned that North Dakota has more than 60 wildlife refuges protecting everything from white pelicans to prairie chickens, plus huge recreational lakes created by the dammed up Missouri River. About one-third of the state's 643,000 residents are of Scandinavian descent, and the town of Mountain in the Red River Valley stages an Icelandic festival each August. The farmers of the state raise barley, flaxseed, wheat and rye.

After Wolf Point, we moved into the Fort Peck Indian Reservation where Sioux Indians live in an area 90 by 40 miles wide. The land was flat and the overcast sky looked like rain.

Montana was prairie land partially planted in wheat. There were few trees and a very big sky. I wanted to take some photos of the landscape, but there was not a single window that opened on the train. We were slowed by work on the tracks, but finally arrived at the east side of Glacier National Park around 1900 hrs.

We checked into the Glacier Park Lodge where I had made reservations many months before, and were put into a basement room reeking of mothballs from winter storage. I protested strongly and we were moved to another room on the second floor which was much nicer.

While we didn't have our own automobile in the park, we were able to get around in a delightful White Motor Company touring car. One of our favorite spots in Glacier National Park was beautiful Lake McDonald.

We picked up the train again four days later and 75 miles west at West Glacier. It came in right on time at 2025.

We had been unable to get another suite and ended up in the handicapped compartment, which turned out to be very nice. It was the last car of the train on the bottom level and had windows on both sides. The orange color scheme was the same, but the toilet and sink were in the same room just separated by a diagonal curtain that closed so someone coming in the door could not see into that area.

We met our new conductor who told us he worked freight for 32 years before he could get on a passenger train. The track was smoother along here. We stopped at Whitefish at 2125, and my husband rushed out with paper towels to clean the outside of our windows. We were given two more complimentary baskets of wine, crackers and nuts, and retired for the night and slept all the way across Idaho.

The final leg of our trip took us over the Cascade Mountains and down along Puget Sound into Washington. It was spectacular scenery. We woke up at 0600, now Pacific Time, and made up the lower bed into two chairs ourselves.

At 0745 we passed Mount Rainier to the south. It sat in majestic splendor, white and shining under a lovely spot of sun. There were green fields, farmhouses, dairy cattle, and finally the towns of Everett and Puget Sound. We saw lumber being loaded onto the Japanese ship *Hirado*.

Puget Sound was a misty gray, and the surrounding hills were bathed in fog. Small fishing boats were leaving port. We passed a beach and saw children digging in the sand while seagulls flew overhead. A patch of blue sky appeared in the far distance.

The snow-covered tops of the distant Olympic Mountains glistened above the fog and below the clouds. We passed a graveyard of rotting boats, their wooden hulls and bows now almost gone.

There were boatyards, oil refineries and storage tanks, driftwood, and people walking their dogs, a steamboat… and the startling announcement over the loudspeaker, "It's Miller time! All passengers detrain at the King Street Station!"

We were in Seattle fifteen minutes early, the sun was shining, and in spite of the frustrations, we had had a marvelous trip.

For up-to-date information:
www.amtrak.com

According to Amtrak publicity, a lot has changed on the *Empire Builder*.
In August 2005 improvements were made which included refurbished rail cars.
"Passengers will be treated to a new onboard experience as the *Empire Builder* travels across eight states from Chicago to Seattle and Portland."
Even the food is said to be better, with ham and English beefsteak pot pie being added to the menu.
The *Empire Builder* now splits/or combines the train in Spokane, Washington, one branch from/to Seattle, the other from/to Portland, OR.
The *Empire Builder* offers daily departures both from Chicago (1415 hrs.) and the West Coast (both Seattle and Portland) which leave at 1645 hrs.

CHAPTER ELEVEN

AMTRAK SPEEDS TRAVELERS TO THE NATION'S CAPITAL IN STYLE
New York to Washington, D.C.
October 1984

Passengers prepare to board AMTRACK in Baltimore.

It is autumn and the leaves have turned to red and gold. Our Amtrak *Metroliner* "flies" through the autumn woods, over rivers and past a dozen cities on its way to the nation's capital. The seats are filled with executive types: men in suits and vests, and women in suits and sensible blouses. All carry the obligatory briefcase. Some work diligently over reports and presentations, and others read the sports pages of the morning's newspapers. A few sleep.

I have been up since 0400 because Amtrak's *Metroliner* leaves New York's Pennsylvania Station at 0600. The ride will take three hours with brief stops in Newark, Metropark, and Trenton, N.J., Philadelphia, PA., Wilmington, Delaware, Baltimore, MD, and into Washington.

There are later trains. *Metroliner* Service is also available leaving New York City at 0705, 0800 and 0900. In between are five more trains with names like *The Pennsylvanian* and *The Bankers.* These trains make several more stops, and their seats are not reserved.

My seat is roomy and comfortable. It is one of two on each side of a wide aisle, all facing forward. It not only has a footrest in front, but a leg-rest which lifts up for comfort when you place the back of your chair in a reclining position.

The color décor of the car is

blue and white; there is blue and white diamond-shaped upholstery, blue tweedy-looking carpeting on the floor and under the windows, plus blue and white window curtains. A touch of color is added at the end of the car where the doors to the restrooms are colored a bright red.

We leave in the darkness and within twelve minutes have stopped in Newark. I can find no signs to tell me where I am, so I ask the conductor. He not only answers my questions, but supplies me with a schedule.

This man from Long Island has been working on railroads for 32 years. He tells me that the train is carrying six cars today with four coach cars capable of carrying sixty people each. We have 263 people scheduled to ride today.

He also shows me the first-class compartment in the front of the train where the seats are upholstered in bright orange, and are all just a bit wider. Passengers are fed a complimentary meal here.

I ask him about the usual number of passengers for the 0600 run to Washington as I have seen many empty seats.

"We will pick up 150 to 175 passengers in Philadelphia," the conductor explains, "and another 40 to 50 in Wilmington."

He believes that this train, which reaches speeds up to 120 miles per hour (190 kph), is popular with business people because it goes all the way into the center of the cities.

"People who fly have to deal with getting in and out of the airports, which is always a time-consuming hassle," he points out.

When I ask him about the condition of the tracks, he says

Union Station in Washington, D.C.

they can be rough because of the freight trains which use the same tracks. "Ten years ago," he continues, "when the equipment was new, we tested it on a stretch of track between New Brunswick and Trenton. It is a top track with no curves, and we ran the train up to 155 mph (248 kph)!"

It is nearly an hour later and we are past Trenton before I see the beginnings of morning light. I decide to buy a cup of coffee and the lead service attendant gives me a food list and explains the food service. A native of Trinidad, he has been working American trains for the past twelve years and can take care of either the club or snack car.

I buy a cup of coffee and a Danish with a raspberry jelly filling which is cold from the refrigerator. The menu shows a variety of sandwiches including a hot dog, and a

ham and Swiss cheese. Beverages include coffee, juice, milk and soft drinks plus beer, wine, and cocktails/liquor.

I learn that food served in the club car to first-class passengers includes a breakfast of cereal, omelets, pancakes, waffles and sausages. For dinner you may order beef short ribs, chicken, lasagna, vegetables, Mexican combo, pasta, chicken salad, crab/shrimp or tuna salad, seafood or turkey.

I take my coffee into a dining car which has eight white Formica tables and seats with comfortable brown cushions. I see out my window several areas of heavy industry and more train tracks. At 0717 hours we pass some trees and go over the Schuykill River where university students are sculling small boats along the river. This area is known as "boat house row" as

WHISTLES, SMOKE & STEAM

several universities have facilities here.

Past the river is a freeway, and then a tunnel. We arrive in Philadelphia and more people crowd aboard. There is a sudden scramble for the dining tables, and I am joined by three railroad engineers, formerly with the Pennsylvania Railroad and now working for Amtrak. The men are going to a celebration commemorating the closing of the last two grade crossings (*where the train tracks cross a road*), in Maryland: the Glendale Grade Crossing and the Hillmeade. The crossings have been replaced by overhead bridges.

The three men are very knowledgeable about railroad history. Collectively they have had more than one hundred years of railroading experience. Their district includes Washington to Boston, Philadelphia to Harrisburg, and New Haven to Springfield, Massachusetts.

They tell me that Amtrak patronage is up approximately seven percent and a $2.2 billion program titled "The Northeast Corridor Improvement Project" is now winding down. It began as a Congressional bill and provided funds for new tracks, new and rehabilitated movable bridges, alignment changes, communication and signal modernization, new and rehabilitated stations, service facilities for locomotive and passenger cars, and installation of many miles of right-of-way fences, an important safety feature along this high-speed corridor.

It is 0745 and we have arrived at the Wilmington station which, like Baltimore, has recently undergone renovation.

"You must stop on your way

back and see the Baltimore station," one of the men tells me. "It is very beautiful with colored glass and a dome skylight."

I learn that there was a high society ball when the Wilmington Station reopened last June to celebrate its being restored to its former grandeur. The Baltimore reopening in the early part of year was commemorated with a black-tie affair sponsored by local patrons. The men seemed very pleased to tell me about it.

0759 - Elkton, MD. "Couples used to come here and get married," one of the men remarks wistfully.

0805 - We cross over the Susquehanna River and pass the town of Havre de Grace, MD. which has many lovely trees. "We'll need a new bridge here within the next twenty years," one man remarks.

The train rushes on past Bush River and Gunpowder, Maryland. It is foggy and we can see very little.

I ask my new engineering friends about Amtrak safety and learn that there is a regular track inspection by a sophisticated track-geometry car once a month. The tracks are also walked twice a week, and a local inspector rides the train. The Federal Railway Administration sends out inspectors, plus there are certain state inspectors.

"Our railroad has never had a bridge collapse because of structure standards," one of the engineer says, "though one might wash away in a catastrophic 100-year flood."

We enter Baltimore and as my new friends have been so enthusiastic about this station restoration, I decide to go and see it (*on the way*

back to New York). The main lobby has three gorgeous domes of colored glass. There are high-back wooden seats with rounded white light globes at the ends, plus white marble pillars and walls. A second waiting room has yellow and green tiles, the same wooden seats and a beautifully-crafted round wooden information booth. Everything is spotlessly clean.

0859 - The passengers of Amtrak's *Metroliner*, train No. 290, arrive right on time in Washington, D.C. at the impressive Union Station for a day of business appointments and sightseeing. It had been a fine ride.

For up-to-date information:
www.amtrak.com

The new Acela Express offers hourly service downtown during peak morning and afternoon rush hours between New York, Washington, DC, and intermediate cities, as well as many convenient round-trips between New York and Boston. Amtrak states, "Enjoy superior comfort, upscale amenities, and polished professional service - at speeds up to 150mph - aboard Acela Express. You will enjoy Reserved or First Class and Business Class seating, at-seat electrical outlets, adjustable lighting and large tray tables. First Class provides at-seat meals and beverage service, hot towel service, a newspaper and access to Club Acela lounges."

Amtrak's *San Joaquin* sits on the tracks in Merced after a four hour run from Oakland, California.

CHAPTER TWELVE

AN AMTRAK RIDE FROM OAKLAND, CALIFORNIA
TO YOSEMITE NATIONAL PARK
April 2002

From the window on the bus I could see patches of snow still lining the highway as we headed up into the Sierras for a spring visit to Yosemite National Park in north-central California. Winter was definitely receding as evidenced by fields of purple lupine, a promise of colorful wildflowers and luscious berries to follow. I smelled the air fresh with the scent of sugar pine forests, eucalyptus trees and manzanita. We were surprised to spot coyotes circling through the woods, and later a

small herd of mule deer.

Looking down into a mountain brook we spied brown trout hidden in the deep shadows of

silent pools. Yosemite is renewed each spring with fresh fields of grass and roaring waterfalls. It was like revisiting an old friend to see once again the magnificent sequoia trees, Half Dome, El Capitan and Yosemite and Bridal Veil Waterfalls. In the spring it is easier to visit these sights and enjoy their tranquility before the rush of summer crowds.

For this visit we chose to arrive in a different way. My husband and I boarded an Amtrak train in Oakland at the Jack London Station. We left right on time at

AMTRACK,
Oakland, California.

1300 hrs for the three-hour trip to Merced, where we connected with a motorcoach for a two-hour ride to the park.

The train, called the *San Joaquin*, was furnished with modern equipment and provided a smooth ride over well-maintained tracks. The seats were blue upholstery accompanied with white trays, foot rests and overhead luggage compartments. Light was provided by long fluorescent lamps running along two sides of the ceiling and small reading lamps.

Our route followed San Pablo Bay, Carqueniz Straits and the Delta, with several stops including Martinez, Antioch, Stockton and Merced. We viewed a stunning amount of wildlife consisting of white egrets, swans, mallards, cinnamon teal, pintail ducks and blue and white heron.

Industrial sights consisted of the U.S. Naval Weapons Depot, the antique C&H Sugar Mill, old train yards and piles of recycled metals along the tracks in Stockton. One fascinating sight was the Castle Air Museum in Atwater for which our conductor slowed the train. We could view old World War II planes, a de Havilland Mosquito Bomber and a Lockheed Black Bird SR 71 reconnaissance jet, once the fastest plane in the world and famous for spying on the Soviet Union.

We arrived in Merced and boarded a motorcoach provided by Via Adventures, Inc. The bus was furnished with cushioned seats, air conditioning and a restroom. They had small TV sets and showed an interesting 20 minute video of the 1997 flood in Yosemite. Walter, our driver, gave us a running commentary of the video and what we

Picnic lunch at the historic Wanona Hotel, Yosemite.

would see once we arrived in Yosemite Valley.

Spring and summer activities in Yosemite included touring various sites by open-air tram, bicycling, river rafting, golfing, horseback riding, swimming, hiking and mountaineering, all of which make Yosemite an ideal destination spot.

It is possible to make a one-day tour to Yosemite by Amtrak and Via Adventures. The train to Yosemite operates daily, leaving Oakland at 0730 and arriving in Merced at 1030. Here the train connects with a motorcoach which brings passengers into the park at 1310. The return journey leaves at 1615 and arrives back in Oakland at 2200 hours.

The trip includes narrated sightseeing, a box lunch, the Yosemite National Park entrance fee, a guided tour of Yosemite Valley by open-air tram (or bus if

the weather is bad), and a full-color Yosemite booklet.

There are also two-day trips and other excursions.

For up-to-date information:
Amtrak California, 800-USA-RAIL (872-7245)
or www.amtrakcalifornia.com
Amtrak's dedicated Amtrak California website.

The *San Joaquin* provides service from Oakland through to Bakersfield.
There is also a bus connection from the San Francisco Ferry Building to Emeryville. Via Adventures, Inc, 300 Grogan Ave., Merced, 1-888-Park Bus (727-5287), 1-800-VIALINE (842-5463) or www.via-adventures.com

Engine #933 at Woolshed Flat, South Australlia

PART 2

Train Excursions
& Tourist Rides,
plus
Oslo, Norway's
Airport Express;
Bergen, Norway's
Floibanen
Funicular Railway;
& San Francisco's
Cable Cars

Airport Express
Train station in
Oslo, Norway

CHAPTER THRITEEN
SCANDINAVIA - TWO NORWAY RAIL RIDES
June 2000 and August 2004

OSLO'S AIRPORT EXPRESS TRAIN

Airport Express Train.

The Airport Express Train from Gardermoen International Airport into Oslo was built in 1998, the same year the new airport opened. It runs a distance of 45 Kilometers (around 30 miles) into town and costs passengers about a fourth of what is charged by taxi drivers to go the same distance.

After boarding the train at the airport, we rode to the second stop to disembark in downtown Oslo. Like all trains, there was a light shaking motion, but on the whole the ride was quite smooth.

The interior of our car was designed with gray walls and blue upholstered seats with flecks of color. The seats faced both forward and backwards. The lighting was soft neon covered with a metal net, and luggage racks were built in the end of each car.

The train, which left every ten minutes, took us through a countryside of green fields and arrived in the city in only nineteen minutes. A TV monitor gave us some useful information on the way, such as the temperature outside and news and stock market reports. There were also advertisements. One announcement on the monitor told tourists to stay away from farm animals because of mad cow disease.

Tickets sold at the airport station were located at counters just before you descend to the trains. Passengers could also slide their credit cards through a machine to pay for their transportation.

Even though I was extremely tired by the time I reached Norway from California, the train ride was comfortable and fun. All the facilities were modern and clean and the entire operation very convenient.

THE FLOIBANEN FUNICULAR RAILWAY
BERGEN, NORWAY

Norway's famous funicular (also called a cable car), which has been running up to Mount Floyen in Bergen since 1918, is the only one of its kind in Scandinavia. Passengers board in the city center, just a couple of blocks from the popular Fish Market.

When we took the ride up, I counted nine rows of seats in each individual car, which rested on the hill like stair steps. These cars, painted red and blue, were new in 2002. Each shoots passengers 320 meters (approximately 1050 feet) straight up and down the mountainside in seven or eight minutes. Our trip up took a little longer as we made three stops to let passengers off. The stops to residential areas were called: Promsgate, Fjellveien and Skansemyren.

The blue car in which we rode both up and down had blue upholstered seats and a gray composite floor. Florescent lights were placed above on the sides. Large panoramic windows and a glass roof gave us spectacular views of the scenery. Aluminum handles were provided for passengers to hold on to if the seats were all taken and some people had to stand.

The total rail track for the funicular was 844 meters long (2,769 feet) and had gradients of 15 to 26 degrees in the steepest part of the climb. The power was provided by 315 KW AC-engines which were operated from the cars via signals transmitted through an inductive cable in the tracks.

Automatic rail brakes would be activated if the speed got too great which would bring the cars to a stop within seconds. Emergency brakes would be activated in the event of any other irregularities.

Bergen Funicular.

Ginger Dingus from California aboard the Funicular train.

The Floibanen Funicular was also provided with diesel-powered back-up engines in case of power failure.

As we started to ascend the mountain, the city of Bergen and surrounding mountains and fjords lay below in a splendid panorama of breathtaking beauty. Farther up we passed through tunnels. Some steps and rock walls were in evidence at each stop, along with well-tended gardens of blooming flowers. Wooden poles along one side supported lights and electric lines.

Half-way up our blue car passed the red car coming down. As we climbed higher and higher, the views stretched out even wider, and the area below looked like a magic city set in sunshine among sparkling blue fjords and green mountains.

At the top there were walks along the edge of the mountainside where passengers enjoyed the view and read displays identifying what they were looking at below. I studied the names of the mountains, fjords and landmarks in the city such as the railway station, areas where the cruise ships docked and the airport. There were also mountain paths and I hiked a little way back down before returning to visit the restaurant and cafeteria, souvenir shop and children's playground area.

A long white wooden restaurant, which contained a café and open-air terrace, was called the Floien Folkerestaurant. Large windows provided diners spectacular views of Bergen far down the mountain. The restaurant was open daily in the summer season — mid May to the end of August. The rest of the year the cafeteria was open weekends from noon to 1700.

The funicular itself operated daily every fifteen minutes throughout the year with slightly longer hours in the summer. Tickets to ride were quite inexpensive with children paying half price.

Top: Lounge car on the
Rovos Rail. Bottom:
Kimberley Club,
KImberley, South Africa.

CHAPTER FOURTEEN

SOUTH AFRICA ABOARD THE ROVOS RAIL
March 1996

Rovas Rail Victorian dining car.

CAPE TOWN, SOUTH AFRICA — The luxurious Rovos Rail's "*Pride of Africa*" links Cape Town to the capital at Pretoria with stops at Matjiesfontein, Kimberley and Johannesburg. Other routes go on to Maputo, Mozambique on the Indian Ocean, Victoria Falls in Zimbabwe and Dar-es-Salaam in Tanzania, as well as Cape Town to Knysna on the south coast.

My husband and I had just finished an extensive wine tour in the Cape region when we boarded this delightful restored railway for a two day (one full and two half-days, plus two nights) journey to

Johannesburg. We found the experience reminiscent of the golden age of trains rivaling the Orient Express, but running through the African bush where railroads once carried gold prospectors, diamonds and ivory.

Today the "commodities" are pampered tourists who sink down in soft cushioned chairs in the comfortable lounge cars sipping drinks and watching the vast African sunsets. The pace is slow, the food and wines delicious and the scenery spectacular.

The *Pride of Africa* carries a maximum of 70 passengers who are all assigned suites. Ours was quite spacious with twin beds pushed together, four large windows, wood-lined cabinets, one small wardrobe plus shelves above, and two black and gold upholstered chairs. A built-in refrigerator was well stocked with sparkling cham-

pagne, wine, beer, chocolates and other snacks. The bedspread had a flowered design and the carpet was a green-and-gold pattern. There were neon overhead lights plus small reading lamps. Our private bath was equipped with a sink, toilet and glass-enclosed shower plus a hair dryer, all of which worked perfectly.

Our send-off in Cape Town was an entertaining event with champagne, orange juice, violins playing and much merriment. Although there was a staggering mountain of luggage brought aboard, every piece eventually found its way to the right suite and a friendly young hostess instructed us on how to turn on the lights, the showers and gave us other pertinent information.

"The company has four steam engines," she explained, "but it is sometimes difficult to put them in

service because many supply stations where water and coal are stored have been abandoned. There is also the danger of fire since the trains cross through the dry African bush."

We left Cape Town being pulled by an electric locomotive which remained until we arrived at De Aar at 0800 the next morning. Here we changed to a diesel.

Our route took us north through the lush South African wine region reminiscent of the Napa Valley in Northern California. We were traveling during the harvest in the fall which is March/April in South Africa. The vineyards were heavy with ripened grapes as we rolled past gentle sloping hills and distant mountains plus several classic Cape Dutch estates and wineries.

In the early evening we stopped in Matjiesfontein, an

Lounge car with glass door and viewing platform.

Diamond pit,
Kimberley, South Africa.

authentic Victorian railway village established over 100 years ago. The heart of the town was the Lord Milner Hotel, an Edwardian structure which once provided refreshments to passengers traveling on the Cape Government Railways. After touring the hotel, we explored an old museum literally stuffed with memorabilia of South African life over the past century. I felt like I was in a time warp.

By morning we had reached the Great Karoo, a high desert situated at about 4000 feet contiguous to the central spine of Africa which stretches all the way to Ethiopia.

We passed scrub bushes, prickly pear cactus, eucalyptus trees, white stucco houses with green roofs and red brick houses. It reminded me very much of Central Australia with lots of sheep, some horses and cattle. The rails became quite shaky.

By noon we were passing through grassland, past giant termite mounds and over a muddy river. Outside our picture windows we saw herds of grazing zebra, weaver bird nests hanging from acacia trees and graceful pairs of black and gray ostriches.

Our next stop was in Kimber-

ley where we toured the old diamond mines and a reconstructed pioneer town. Our guide gave us a little history of the area. "Five mines were started with picks and shovels, and one pit is the largest handmade hole in the world," he explained. "14,504,566 karats of diamonds were taken out!"

For a feeling of authenticity, a few artificial "diamonds" had been scattered along a scenic trail where we walked. We had arrived on a Sunday and all the diamond shops were closed causing my husband, and a few others, to celebrate.

Back on the train we were

Old steam
locomotive exhibit
in Kimberley, South Africa.

instructed to dress up for dinner, and while I did not see anyone wearing tuxedos, dark suits and elegant party dresses were prevalent. This was a big contrast to the shorts we had been wearing during the day. The dining car, built in 1924 in Pretoria, had been christened "Shangani," and was Victorian in character with seven pairs of carved wooden, roof-supporting pillars and arches. The car seated 44 passengers.

The tables were set with white table cloths, china, crystal, and fresh flowers, and the menus gave passengers several choices. I enjoyed an entree of lamb one night which was especially tender and juicy. Breakfast offered choices of bacon, eggs, cereals, rolls, fresh fruit, pancakes, juices, coffee and tea.

While the "*Pride of Africa*" went on to Pretoria, we disembarked in Johannesburg to connect with a safari at the Londolozi Game Lodge within the Sabi Sand Reserve adjoining the Kruger National Park. It had been an exciting adventure and I would like to return someday and ride the *Pride of Africa* from Cape Town all the way to Dar-Es-Salaam.

For up-to-date information:
www.rovos.co.za

Rovos Rail now has five steam engines. "The Royal Suites, each of which takes up half a carriage, are named after colourful characters of the Victorian era in South Africa, including Cecil John Rhodes, Barney Barnato and Alfred Beit. Spacious and elegant, the Royal Suites measure 16 sq. metres in size (172 sq. ft.). Each has its own private lounge area and full bathroom with Victorian bath and separate shower."

US Representative - Henry Kartagener, Tel: 1-631-858-1270; Fax: 1-631-858-1279. Email: rovosrail@kainyc.com

CHAPTER FIFTEEN

SOUTH AUSTRALIA'S CORNUCOPIA OF STEAM
June 1990

Engine #933 prepares to leave Woolshed Flat for return trip to Quorn.

QUORN, SOUTH AUS-TRALIA — The state of South Australia can brag of over one hundred and fifty-five years of railroading, and although their original steam trains are long gone, preservation groups have sprung up providing authentic shortened versions of the original runs.

Prominent among these organizations are SteamRanger, which runs excursions south from Adelaide to Victor Harbor, and the Pichi Richi Railway operating out of Quorn.

SteamRanger, the railway operating arm of the Australian Railway Historical Society in South Australia, also operates the popular Cockle Train from Goolwa to Port Elliot and Victor Harbor. Then it gets better: steam enthusiasts can connect with a steamboat in Goolwa which provides fabulous excursions on the Murray River.

STEAMRANGER

The tracks were being repaired for the SteamRanger's *Southern Encounter*, which ran down from Adelaide to Victor Harbor, when I visited in 1990. I had to be content with a tour of the 600' railway shed at Dry Creek, just north of Adelaide, but viewing all the superb equipment turned out to be well worth the trip.

Ian Johnston, an industrial chemist and a SteamRanger volunteer, showed me through some fascinating wide gauge rolling stock.

Their 200 ton #520 express locomotive (4-8-4) "*Sir Malcolm Barclay-Harvey*," was named after a former governor who served South Australia in the 1930s. It was built by the Islington Workshops in Adelaide in 1943 and painted a shining green with yellow trim.

Another locomotive of which SteamRanger was particularly proud was the 140 ton *Duke of Edinburgh*, #621 (4-6-2), also built in Islington in 1936. It was overhauled in 1988 and used to pull Prince Charles and Princess Diana on a visit between Victor Harbor

Quorn, South Australia
Railway Station.

and Goolwa. It is now called the *Royal Engine*.

While the *Duke of Edinburgh* used to speed along at fifty and sixty mph, SteamRanger runs it at 45 mph. The locomotive is capable of pulling six cars up through Mt. Lofty or about fifteen cars on the level.

SteamRanger had four steam locomotives, four diesel electric locomotives, and around thirty carriages that were operational, plus some spares. The timber-bodied carriages were built around 1910, while the steel cars were from the 1930s.

The Society itself was all voluntary and numbered around 500. Between twenty and fifty members did all the actual work. Ian Johnston said it takes about twelve months to refurbish a broad-gauge carriage.

The handsome 1930's tavern car was modified in 1984 at a cost

of $50,000. It is used for charters such as tours north through he Barossa Valley, famous for wine production.

Some of the 1930's standard carriages, which have center aisles, were bought from the government railroad at a cost of $12,000 each. The Finniss Sleeping Car is SteamRanger's top of the line. It contains a small lounge and can sleep eighteen with two to a compartment. The car has shining chrome sinks, silver fixtures, beveled mirrors and beautifully-polished wood,

Excursions on the *Southern Encounter* on the Victor Harbor Tourist Railway were held every Sunday from September through November plus on additional holidays. Passengers left the outskirts of Adelaide at 9:00 a.m. and returned at 8:00 p.m. Stops were made at Goolwa and Victor Harbor. The run itself took 3 1/2 hours each way

and connected with the paddle wheel steamboat, *P.S. Mundoo*.

COCKLE TRAIN

The broad-gauge *Cockle Train* ran for eleven miles (17 km) between Goolwa, Port Elliot and Victor Harbor along the south coast of the Fleurieu Peninsula. This picturesque trip crossed farmlands and coastal dunes along the blue waters of the Southern Ocean.

The train had been named for the cockles it carried from Goolwa Beach to resale outlets along the coast. It ran during the holiday season between the 1890s and the 1920s. The run today is still picturesque as quite a lot of the track follows the sea.

In 1986, SeamRanger upgraded the operation, spending 2.4 million dollars. The train is pulled by an RX class #224 (4-6-0) built in Queensland in 1915 by Waulers

Brill Model 75 Railcar, Pichi Richi Railway. Quorn, South Australia.

South Australian Railway Commissioner's Carriage, "Flinders," a real beauty with "leather" seats, polished wood paneling, beveled glass and carpeting. In its day the car could sleep eight plus attendants. General Douglas McArthur used this car during the Second World War to travel part of his long journey from Melbourne to Darwin.

The Pichi Richi Railway runs on some of the last of the 3'6" narrow gauge railway left in South Australia. Their mainstay locomotives are comparatively modern steam engines built in the early 1950s and are quite large for a narrow-gauge track.

On the day I took an excur-

Limited.

When a fireban is declared for the Mt. Lofty Ranges District, the *Cockle Train* operates with a diesel locomotive.

PICHI RICHI RAILWAY

The one-thousand member Pichi Richi Railway Preservation Society operates out of Quorn, 220 miles north of South Australia's capital city of Adelaide. Founded in 1973, over five hundred of these enthusiastic members can be counted upon to join the "parties" that do the actual restoration work. Their results are most impressive.

The organization has purchased over one hundred pieces of rolling stock, much of which is kept under shelter. They run regularly-scheduled excursions over part of the 10 miles of track to a place called Woolshed Flat where passengers can picnic. They

Geoff Horne, cab driver, engine #933, Pichi Richi Railway.

also provide workshop/museum tours of their facilities at Quorn and can arrange for private parties to travel in a historic lounge car. This car is none other than the ex-

sion, the locomotive was #933 W, an ex-WAGR W-Class (4-8-2), mixed traffic locomotive built by Beyer-Peacock in England in 1951. It pulled eight cars containing 180 passengers. The capacity was 250.

The carriage I rode in was built by the South Australian Railway at

Max Atkinson, guard on the Pichi Richi Railway.

Hammond, Carrieton and Ororoo for some thirty years. Built in England in 1905, this steam motor coach consists of a small saturated locomotive-type boiler and cab fitted on a four-wheel underframe. The engine was built in Leeds, while the coach was manufactured in Birmingham.

The inside of the "Coffee Pot" was divided into first-and-second class compartments and was beautifully restored with polished woods, including English oak, Klinki pine and teak. Black mock leather seats, plush floral red-and-gold carpeting, louvered wood shutters, brass light fixtures and net luggage racks completed the décor.

For up-to-date information on SteamRanger and the Cockle Train: www.steamranger.org.au

For information on the Pichi Richi Railway: www.prr.org.au or www.flindersranges.com

STEAMRANGER
Southern Encounter now originates at Mt. Barker and travels to Victor Harbor in the morning and returns in the afternoon. Travel time is about 2 1/2 hours.

PICHI RICHI RAILWAY
Steam Motor coach No. 1, affectionately known as the "Coffee Pot," celebrated its 100th anniversary in 2006. It ran a series of luncheon specials before being retired for a major overhaul.

the Adelaide Locomotive Workshops in 1888. Thirty-six identical carriages were built there between 1883-1899. They had first-and-second-class compartments, plus special ladies and smoking compartments. The longitudinal seating allowed for fourteen passengers in First Class and 25 in Second. After 1895, a lavatory was put into one side of the central compartment. Westinghouse air brakes were installed in Quorn in 1912.

The car was rebuilt in 1981 and returned to passenger use in 1983. It had padded leather longitudinal seats, seven square windows on each side, mahogany paneling, a white curved ceiling and two light fixtures with three bulbs in each.

While the round-trip was listed at two hours-and-fifty minutes, we took well over three hours as there was a film crew aboard. We also spent some extra time at the picnic area know as Woolshed Flat where refreshments were sold from a refreshment carriage.

The Pichi Richi Railway also operates a priceless little piece of equipment called the "Coffee Pot" which once ran between Quorn and Hawker, Port Augusta,

CHAPTER SIXTEEN

RAIL TRIP AND EXCURSIONS EXPLORE SIGHTS IN NORTHERN SPAIN
June 1988

El Transcantabrico crosses a bridge at Navia, Spain.

Bar Car on the El Transcantabrico.

LEON, SPAIN — The splendid blue and ivory *El Transcantabrico* (pronounced El Trans-can-tab'-bree-ko), is a scenic tourist train running 625 miles through Northern Spain and the longest narrow gauge line in Europe. Since 1983 it has been operated from June through the second week of October by FEVE, Spain's Narrow Gauge Railway Company, Ferrocarriles de Via Estrecha.

Sprinkled along the route between Leon and Ferrol are ancient cities which were once stops along a pilgrimage trail, picturesque fishing villages, rolling green hills, soaring mountains with sheer limestone cliffs, rivers, parks, and finally, the dazzling blue Cantabrico Sea.

Throughout the trip, passengers disembark the train to explore archaeological and artistic treasures such as a 2000-year-old Roman villa, lofty Gothic cathedrals, medieval inns and Romanesque churches. Most of these attractions are reached by a comfortable Mercedes Benz bus which accompanies *El Transcantabrico* the entire week of its tour.

The train itself is a delight. Because it is narrow gauge (one meter wide or 39.37 U.S. inches), the coaches are smaller than the regular standard gauge, but well-

Fishing village of Luarca, Spain.

planned for as much comfort as possible.

The nine cars consist of the engine, energy coach (helper engine) which also carries water, four sleeping coaches, and three public cars: the Saloon, Pub and Bar Cars.

The diesel locomotive is an Alsthon, one of nine diesel engines built in Barcelona with French technology in 1984. The engines, grey with red and orange stripes, are numbered #1650 through #1658. During the week that I was a passenger on the *El Transcantabrico*, I was invited to ride in engine #1652 for one and a-half hours from Cabezon de la Sal to the seaside town of Llanes. Inside this diesel locomotive was a black control panel containing gauges, knobs, dials, a steering wheel, foot pedals and lights of red, green, blue, yellow and white.

One gauge registered our speed which averaged 45 kilometers per hour (28 mph) but actually ran between 25 and 50. Another noted the water, and a third was identified as a tachometer which recorded the revolutions of the motor per minute. Two dials gave information on the locomotive and train brakes, while a wheel was used as a clutch to slow the train. Two fans were attached overhead to keep the space cool.

Our engineer, Antonio Bolongo, was a five-year employee who had been a "locomotive driver" for two years. His training consisted of two-and-a-half years of learning on the job as an assistant engineer.

He explained, "The foot pedals are a safety feature in case the engineer is suddenly incapacitated, such as having a heart attack. The driver," he continued, "has to push the pedals every fifteen seconds or a bell will ring to remind him. Then he has three seconds to push them or the train will start to slow down."

Antonio showed us his time schedule which he followed to the minute and explained about the track lights, signs and signals. "This S ('Silbar' in Spanish is 'whistle') next to the track means the engineer should blow the whistle, which is done by pushing this knob situated to the left of the wheel. One long blast sounds when we are ready to leave or before a crossing, and two short blasts alone mean the train is backing up."

He demonstrated with a short blast on the whistle, then continued. "A green light ahead shines when all is clear, while orange warns of a stop coming up. Station masters will also appear with red batons outside each depot to wave us by."

It was raining slightly when we pulled out at 1725 and the windshield wiper was moving slowly. We rode out of town passing small houses covered with pink roses and

51

The beach at Santander.

into the green countryside. The train entered a tunnel and emerged on a curve where the banks were covered with wildflowers. The rain poured harder as we continued through a series of tunnels, one of 799 meters (873.79 yards) long.

When we arrived at a place called "Vidiago," the train crossed over a high railroad bridge and we stopped midway on this high trestle where we were allowed exactly two minutes to jump off and take a few quick photos.

Continuing on through the hills, we crossed another bridge spanning the Tinamagor River, the boundary between the regions of Cantabria and Asturias, before finally arriving in Llanes.

While the ride in the engine was the highlight of my train adventure, I spent many happy hours in the air-conditioned public cars. All three, built in England in 1913, had been operated in the Basque country and had been total-

ly abandoned when they were rescued and restored for the *El Transcantabrico*.

The Pub Car was situated at the end of the train and contained a bar (not in use on our trip), an electric organ and a tape cassette player. The music was wired to speakers for sound in all three public cars.

The curtains and upholstered chairs were rust-colored and the carpet tan. A shiny brown formica-type material was used for the eight tables and occasionally on the walls.

The next car up was the "Saloon," which was furnished with ten tables, each with a small brass lamp and two chairs. There were also six tan upholstered chairs for watching television. (One day I heard the "Golden Girls" speaking Spanish and it must have translated well, for all the women were laughing uproariously). The window curtains in the Saloon Car were rust-

striped and the floor was covered with a tan carpet.

The third car up which contained the "Bar" was reserved for non-smokers. Besides the bar, it was furnished with five tables, also with brass lamps, and tan upholstered chairs. The carpet was a gray/pink-checked design.

A small library of books, magazines, and newspapers was set up at the opposite end from the bar. A map showing our route was pinned up here along with a daily schedule.

The only meal which we ate on the train was breakfast, which was served between approximately 0830 and 1030 hrs in the Bar and Saloon Cars. It was cheerful to walk into the Bar Car in the morning and be greeted with a bouquet of carnations plus baskets of fresh oranges, pears, apples and bananas. The tables were covered with bright orange linen tablecloths and napkins. The ceilings of the three cars were outfitted with vents and painted a light tan.

Our waiter, also named Antonio, would hustle to bring us large cups of steaming coffee or tea, orange juice, pastries and yogurt. We would pick out our own fruit, and he would deliver it to us on a white plate emblazoned with the *El Transcantabrico* emblem, a black signature against a gold-colored diamond. The wine and juice glasses had this same emblem etched on one side.

In the late afternoons, these cars became a favorite meeting place for cocktails, card playing, TV or just watching the scenery glide by.

At night, an excellent young musician and composer, Antonio Gamaza Vazquez, entertained us at the organ with music for dancing or his own classical pieces. We also played cassette tapes and tried to learn Flamenco dancing. These activities would go on until the wee hours, which is the Spanish tradition of late meals and then all-night partying. One had to learn to sneak in a short siesta during the afternoon.

The four sleeping cars were built in Barcelona and Bilbao in 1954 using German technology. Each car contained one compartment which would open into another to make a double. My cabin contained two bunks in which you could sit up without bumping your head, orange blankets, tiny pillows, a reading light, and individually-controlled heat. A hidden sink appeared when you lifted a lid. Above that was a medicine cabinet with a mirror on the inside door which lit up.

The carpet in the cabin was brown, and the window at the end of my bed was covered with a brown curtain which I could open with my toes while lying in bed. When the sink light was on, I could see my reflection in the shiny swirled/marble material which covered the bottom of the top bunk. I could also reach all of five tiny drawers by just sitting up. One contained a chamber pot in case you did not feel like walking to the WC next door, or down to the end of the hall during the night.

Clothes could be hung on two hooks on the wall, behind the door or in a tiny locked closet at the end of the car. Suitcases were stored under the bottom bunk along with the ladder used to reach the upper berth.

Other features included two plugs with 220 double prong out-

lets, along with glass and bottle holders beside the bed. While there were no built-in alarm clocks, a wake-up service was provided each morning when someone walked through the halls ringing a bell.

Each of the four sleeping coaches contained eight cabins, two toilets and two showers with wooden slat floors. Fresh towels were given to passengers at the beginning of the trip and once midweek.

The halls that ran through the sleeping cars were painted orange on the side of the windows. By facing forward, I found the passageways just wide enough for my hips and one flat hand. Most men had to turn sideways to pass.

The *El Transcantabrico* hosted thirty-five passengers on our trip, eighteen English and seventeen Spanish-speaking. They came from Spain, all over the United States, Switzerland and England. One couple living in Barcelona had originated from Argentina and Norway. Another man had immigrated from Czechoslovakia to Switzerland.

We were given information in both Spanish and English, but the English was halting and of little use. Most of the English-speaking group headed for local tourist offices for brochures and studied guidebooks for information.

The route of our train journey

began in Leon in the province of Castilla-Leon, headed northeast to Palencia, then west past coastal villages in the provinces of Cantabria, Asturias and Galicia to the city of Ferrol. A spectacular side trip was provided by bus into the mountains called "Picos de Europe," or "Peaks of Europe," and the trip ended with a final bus ride to the city of Santiago de Compostela.

Meals, except for breakfast, were provided by selected local restaurants, inns and Paradores — which are Spanish government-run hotels of historical or scenic value.

The actual train trip began at 1910 hrs on a Saturday evening and ended at 0920 the following Saturday morning. The train did not move at night, which helped everyone to sleep.

We had arrived from Madrid by train the day before our journey began, spent the night in the ancient Parador Hotel de San Marcos, then toured Leon before boarding the train around 1800.

Our final train ride on day eight ran from 0725 to 0920, when we arrived in Ferrol and boarded a bus for the two-hour ride to Santiago de Compostela, the end of the pilgrim's journey.

For up-to-date information:

www.spanish-rail.co.uk/trains/transcantabrico.html.
www.transcantabrico.feve.es/ing - Direct link to FEVE and the train

Suites are now available containing a double bed, a minibar, wardrobe, writing desk and telephone with an external line. Each has a private bathroom with hydro-sauna, turbo-massage, steam-bath and hair-dryer. Air-conditioning and heating can be regulated individually.

CHAPTER SEVENTEEN

THE WILLIAM TELL EXPRESS IN SWITZERLAND
July 1990

William Tell Express.

On a trip to Switzerland one year, I was invited to try the Swiss Federal Railway travel package which combined a train and steamboat ride running between "tropical" Lugano in Southern Switzerland, to Lucerne, a medieval city nestled in the northern foothills of the St. Gotthard Pass.

Both cities are built along the shores of dramatically beautiful lakes and offer visitors splendid panoramic views of the water, plus all of the related activities such as swimming, boating, water skiing, and windsurfing.

Lugano, the sunniest spot in Switzerland, in the southeast *canton* (state) of Ticino, combines all the finest in Swiss efficiency with the warmth and friendliness of Italy. Visitors can enjoy the combination of Swiss precision and security plus a warm climate, an easygoing lifestyle and marvelous Italian cooking.

This city, situated on the "Swiss Riviera," is adjacent to the Northern Italian lake region and has often been compared to Rio de Janeiro. Its sparkling blue lake, surrounded by luxury hotels, has cone-shaped mountains which jut out of the water like Rio's Sugar Loaf.

Lucerne, 124 miles north on the train line, is an 800-year-old medieval city. It contains a restored old town with narrow cobbled streets, churches, towers and two covered wooden bridges.

The longest is the Chapel Bridge, which is lined with colorful boxes of flowers and decorated with gabled paintings depicting the history of Lucerne, mainly old war scenes. This bridge is built diagonally across the River Reuss in the very heart of the city and offers pedestrians spectacular views of the old town. Situated next to the Chapel Bridge is the impressive 1333 octagonal stone water tower,

A view of the Swiss countryside from the *William Tell Express*.

a landmark of Lucerne.

The one-day *William Tell Express* can be started in either Lugano or Lucerne. From Lugano, you board the electric train at 0945. I went a bit early and shipped my luggage through to the train station in Lucerne so I wouldn't have to be bothered with it during the trip.

The lounge cars of the *William Tell Express* were located right behind the locomotive. They contained tables covered with white linen tablecloths surrounded by red leather chairs. In the middle of each car was a TV camera which projected the route from a "telecamera" attached to the locomotive in front.

The route took us north with short stops at Bellinzona, Basca, Faido, Airolo, Goschenen, Erstfeld and finally Fluelen, where we

departed the train to board a paddle-wheel steamboat.

Between Airolo and Goschenen, we passed through the famous St. Gotthard Tunnel, 3780' at the highest point and nine miles long.

The scenery on this part of the trip was spectacular, with wide sweeping valleys nestled below snow-covered mountain peaks. The villages we rushed by contained stone churches with tall steeples and terraced vineyards. Outside the towns were waterfalls cascading down the mountains, high bridges and spiral-shaped tunnels.

We transferred to our boat on Lake Lucerne at Fluelen around noon and were immediately ushered into the dining room for lunch. While regular boat passengers can pick from an extended menu, *William Tell Express* passen-

gers had a fixed menu. It consisted of vegetable soup, a stew of beef and carrots, polenta and ice cream. All drinks cost extra.

The boat itself, the *D.S. UnterWalden*, was built in Zurich in 1902 and had been refurbished in 1949, 1961, and between 1983 and 1985. It was one of five paddle-wheel steamboats on Lake Lucerne and could carry 800 passengers. Besides day trips, there were evening cruises which provided music and dancing during the months of July and August.

While the lake was overcast on the day we cruised, the beauty of the boat itself was stunning. The dining hall had panels of exquisitely carved wood paneling, white ceilings with gold trim and green velvet seats. The tables were covered with white linen cloths.

On the upper decks, the wood-

Swiss train on the way to Lucerne.

en benches were painted a peach color. A blue and white triangular flag was attached to a tall steel mast, while an oversized red and white flag of Switzerland flew off the stern.

Graceful swans could be seen swimming on the lake, while sea gulls followed the boat looking for handouts. Along the shores, Alpine houses with steep roofs, wooden beams, balconies and boxes of red geraniums looked out at the lake.

In the heart of the boat, the old red-painted steam engine was situated in full view so passengers could watch it work its magic. The paddle wheels, located on each side of the boat, were out of sight except for little round windows where people could peek through

to watch them turn.

The boat made eleven stops on its leisurely trip up the lake to the city of Lucerne. We finally arrived in this fascinating place at 1500.

On the reverse trip, passengers board the steamboat at 1125 in Lucerne, transfer to the train around 1500 and arrive at the Lugano train at 1712. In the winter months, a motorboat may run instead of a paddle wheel steamer.

The *William Tell* offers the trip

on a paddle steamer in first class, and the train journey in first or second-class air-conditioned coaches. Reservations are compulsory and includes seats on the boat and train, the Swiss lunch, as well as a detailed journey documentation and a souvenir.

The *William Tell Express* operates only from May to October.
www.raileurope.com/us/rail/specialty/william_tell.htm
For more up-to-date information go to:
www.Google.com and put in *William Tell Express*.
I was able to download around ten sites on the train and historic paddle steamers. One was: www.europeanvacation.com/trains/William.htm

Tourists have replaced gold seekers riding the White Pass and Yukon Route from Skagway, Alaska over the 3,000 foot White Pass Summit into the Canadian Yukon.

CHAPTER EIGHTEEN

ALASKA - THE PAST AND THE FUTURE
The White Pass & Yukon Route and the The Midnight Sun Express

THE WHITE PASS AND YUKON ROUTE
September 1990

White Pass and
Yukon Route

Skagway, situated at the north end of the Lynn Canal, is the head of navigation in the waters of southeastern Alaska. It was the seaward terminus of the White Pass and Yukon railway, which brought many thousands of people and supplies to the gold fields during the Klondyke Rush in the Canadian Yukon. Built in 1898-1900, this historic line, took 26 months to complete as it was literally blasted through coastal mountains. The project required tens of thousands of men and 450 tons of explosives to complete what

was considered an impossible task.

The route climbs around 3000 feet and features 3.9 degree grades in just twenty miles. There are turns of sixteen degrees, two tunnels, and a steel cantilever bridge completed in 1901. The final route ran 110 miles connecting Skagway, Alaska to Whitehorse, Yukon and into northwest Canada.

The railroad closed due to low mineral prices in 1982 and was reopened in 1988 as a seasonal tourist operation. Now called the White Pass and Yukon Route, The Scenic Railway of the World, it car-

ries around 300,000 tourist passengers annually up the valley of the Skagway River to the summit of White Pass and down the Canadian side to Fraser, B.C., where the riders board a bus for the trip to Whitehorse.

I rode this train as a side trip while taking the Alaska ferries down the Inside Passage. We went from Skagway up over the 3,000 foot White Pass Summit into the Yukon. There were spectacular panoramas of the Saw Tooth Mountains and the Lynn Canal, a deep and narrow arm of the sea

The White Pass and Yukon Route railroad was built with British financing amounting to ten million dollars between 1898-1900, using Canadian contracting and American engineering.

thrust far up between stunning mountain ranges. Riding in vintage parlor cars, we passed rushing torrents of water, cascading waterfalls, trestles and craggy mountainsides. I remember some areas as having very steep drop-offs below the tracks which made the ride very exciting and a little scary. There were names like Pitchfork Falls, Tunnel Mountain, Inspiration Point and Dead Horse Gulch. We stayed overnight in Whitehorse, though it would have been possible to immediately take the bus back to Skagway.

I learned that this railroad was built in spite of great odds against it and is considered one of the engineering marvels of its time. It was completed with British financing amounting to ten million dollars, Canadian contracting and American engineering. Its purpose was to haul miners and supplies over the lofty pass between

Skagway and the Yukon. The gold rush was on and people were hiking the Chilkoot Trail to try and seek their fortunes.

One of the railroad steam engines was #40 from the Baldwin Locomotive Works which was used on the International Railway of Central America. Later it was sold to the Colorado Central Narrow Gauge Railway Co., and operated in Central City from 1970-1976. It was then used for a while on the Georgetown Loop Railroad.

In July 2005 Engine No. 69 arrived in Skagway to be used on the railroad, a 1907 Baldwin 2-8-0, the largest steam locomotive ever made for the WP&YR and a marvel of the restoration skills of dedicated men.

The season for the White Pass and Yukon Route runs from the middle of May through most of September with a 52-miles-roundtrip to Fraser Meadows

which takes four hours; a combined train and bus trip from Skagway to Whitehorse, Yukon, about five hours one way; an eight and 1/2 hour roundtrip to Lake Bennett; and a three and-a-half hour White Pass Summit Excursion. Both steam and diesel locomotives are used to pull the trains.

The White Pass & Yukon Route was designated an International Historic Civil Engineering Landmark in 1994. This is an honor shared by only 36 world civil engineering marvels, such as the Eiffel Tower, Statue of Liberty and the Panama Canal.

For the latest information:
www.whitepassrailroad.com
call 1-800-343-7373.
www.whitepassrailroad.com/schedule.html
Lists current excursions

THE MIDNIGHT SUN EXPRESS
May 1991

Passengers board the *Midnight Sun Express.*

Another popular train ride for tourists exploring Alaska is the sleek *Midnight Sun Express*. I joined a group to ride in an Ultra Dome for an eight-hour railroad excursion from Denali National Park to Anchorage. We rode 356 miles past homesteaders' cabins, farmlands, bush airstrips and just plain open space. We were told to watch for moose but did not see any. Once we saw a view of Mt. McKinley.

While this Alaska railroad will not break any speed records because permafrost affects the smoothness of the railroad tracks, the scenery was beautiful and the accommodation luxurious.

Princess Tours operates four of these domed cars, which are reportedly the largest passenger cars anywhere in the world. They are designed with large curved safety glass panels which are tinted on top to defuse ultraviolet rays from the sun and keep the interior cool.

The 90-or-so passengers on board the day I traveled sat at private oak tables with soft cushioned seats. All cars were fully heated and air-conditioned. For passengers who desired some fresh air, there was even an open platform in back.

The young people who staffed the *Midnight Sun Express* served drinks in the Ultra Dome cars, while dinner was provided on the lower level with tables featuring linen tablecloths and fine china. The menu offered such selections as smoked salmon mousse, prawn cocktail, prime rib, Arctic seafood, chicken dijonaise, lasagna, lamb and scampi. Everyone enjoyed their dinner, and even the desserts were delicious.

For up-to-date information:

Cruise Web handles information on all the Princess Ships
and you can call direct at:
1-800-377-9383.
www.midnightsunexpress.com

Cowboy performers serenade passengers with Western songs on the Grand Canyon Railway

CHAPTER NINETEEN

ARIZONA GRAND CANYON RAILWAY
October 2004

Shoot-out at Grand Canyon Railway Hotel in Williams before the train leaves for the Canyon.

WILLIAMS, ARIZONA — The rebirth and growth of the Grand Canyon Railway is an amazing feat which has been celebrated by hundreds of thousands of rail fans from around the world since the line's reopening in 1989. My sister and I took a ride on the train the last Saturday in October and were astonished by a crowd of 611 eager passengers that late in the year. Three locomotives and a power car were needed to pull twelve passenger cars up to the Grand Canyon and back to Williams, Arizona, an outing that lasted seven hours and forty-five minutes. Since it was Fall, the leisure season, our train was pulled by three diesel engines. Steam locomotives are used only in the summer from Memorial Day through Labor Day.

The Grand Canyon Railway was originally a branch of the Atchison, Topeka and Santa Fe Railroad, and was built to haul copper ore from mines south of the canyon and passengers to the canyon. It began operation on September 17, 1901 and continued for 67 years, though train equip-ment was requisitioned in the early 1940s for government use during World War II.

The demise of the railway began after a road for vehicles was built in 1927. That year 70,382 passengers arrived by train. By 1933, out of 73,034 visitors to the park, only 11,239 rode the Grand Canyon Railway (Santa Fe) to the South Rim. Still, the line managed to hang on until 1968 when only three passengers rode the last run from Williams to the canyon.

The situation looked pretty dismal for the next twenty-one

years and railfans thought all was lost. The tracks, railroad stations and equipment deteriorated year after year. Finally, the railroad equipment was scheduled to be sold for salvage. Then a miracle happened. On January 10, 1989, Max and Thelma Biegert, the new principals of the Grand Canyon Railway, made an announcement that the train would reopen in just seven months.

Seventeen Pullman Standard Harriman-style passenger cars built in 1923 which had been in use on a Southern Pacific commute run from San Jose to San Francisco and Richmond, California, were purchased that January and sent to the Pacific Fruit Express car yards in Tucson, Arizona for restoration.

The sixty-four mile, 4' 8 1/2" tracks were in terrible shape, but an inspired crew rebuilt them in just five months. The newly-revised company also began purchasing loco-motives and other pas-senger cars which could be restored. The Grand Canyon Railway met their announced deadline and the maiden run of the restored line occurred on September 17, 1989. Thousands of rail buffs and local citizens turned out to cheer, both in Williams and the Grand Canyon.

Though the first few years of the railroad's operation did not break even, its success now has been phenomenal. In 2003, 190,000 passen-gers rode between Williams and the Grand Canyon. This also saved

50,000 vehicles from entering the Grand Canyon National Park.

Over the years, more equip-ment has been restored, railroad stations rebuilt, the old Fray Marcos Hotel turned into a histori-cal museum and a new hotel built in Williams.

A tremendous effort went into restoring steam engine #4960, a 2-8-2 Mikado type Baldwin built in Philadelphia in 1923. It had run on the Chicago, Burlington and Quincy railroad, and was pur-chased in 1989, though repairs did not start for another four years. The restoration took three years, 80,000 man-hours and 1.6 million dollars to complete.

Our train eased into the Williams station at 0825 on Saturday, October 30, 2004. I hur-ried out from breakfast to take some photos and saw it was being

pulled by three green diesel engines, all FPA-4 models built by American Locomotive Company in 1959. The engines, numbering 6776, 6773, and 6793, had been purchased from the Canadian National Railway. Following the locomotives, there was a power car which provided electrical power for the train passenger cars.

Next were several of the 1923 Harriman-style Pullman coach cars which had been beautifully restored with green velvet cushions on seats that had room for two passengers on each side of an aisle. Matching green shades were pulled down over the windows, and the ceilings were painted white with white lights and fans. Original mahogany wood paneling and doors had also been restored, which gave each car a classic look. The painted floors were made of four inches of poured

Passengers enjoy the scenery from an observa-tion car on the Grand Canyon Railway

cement. Gold stripes bordered with red decorated the outside of the cars' aluminum bodies. The coach cars were painted a Pullman Green.

The train also had a Pullman Club Car to which a mahogany bar had been added. Two first-class air-conditioned observation cars, the "Coconino" and "Kokapelli Cars," featured small upper-level glass-enclosed domes, and had been furnished with deep red velvet seats and floral carpet on the floor and walls.

The first-class air-conditioned car I rode in, called the "Arizona," had roomy reclining seats with blue upholstery. There were large tinted windows and fluorescent lights which ran along the top. Racks placed above provided ample space for coats and luggage. Serving trays, like those in an airplane, came down in front of each seat.

The café car contained a snack bar with several tables and signs which said that tables could be used for fifteen minutes only and that no card playing was allowed. There was also a good-sized souvenir shop.

I made friends with Bernie Heimenz, the brakeman, who told me he also traded positions with the conductor. Bernie escorted me into the air-conditioned parlor car at the end of the train which was only open to anyone who purchased the higher-priced tickets. The parlor car had small couches and leather upholstered chairs facing in toward the center aisle, plus tiny round tables for food and drinks. It also had an open-air rear platform which, in my opinion, except for riding in the locomotive, was the best spot on the train. I loved the feel of the wind in my

hair and seeing the beautiful high desert and ponderosa pines. It was terrific to be able to photograph the scenery without having a glass window in the way.

I found later you could open windows a little way in the coach and club cars, but they were heavy. Bernie later opened two windows on a platform between cars for me so I could shoot some pictures of the outside of the train curving through Coconino Canyon in the Kaibab Forest.

Each of the cars was staffed by a passenger service attendant. In first-class cars they served fresh fruit, pastries, coffee, tea and juice on the trip up. Coach Class was provided with soft drinks while first-class was served champagne on the way back, plus plates of cheese, nuts, and other snacks. The first-class cars, including the observation

Old Number Eighteen at the Grand Canyon Railway Hotel and Station in Williams is covered with Christmas lights and looks great, although she has not moved in 10 years.

cars and the parlor car, also sold mixed drinks. All the cars had tiny rest rooms in the back.

Our day started out in Williams at the Grand Canyon Railway Hotel with a wild west show at 0930 in a specially-built corral which had a backdrop of wooden store fronts. Six cowboys belonging to the Cataract Creek Gang, led by Two Feathers, staged a fight over who was going to pay for breakfast. Guns were soon blazing and everyone ended up "dead." The show lasted a half-hour and put everyone in a jolly mood.

We boarded the train at 1000 hrs for our two hour and-fifteen-minute ride over sixty-five miles of track through classic Old West territory. No billboards and few telephone wires marred the beauty of this high desert, which was covered in a blanket of snow. It was a journey back in time as we passed through canyons and pinion and juniper woodlands. I learned we were traveling through the world's largest stand of ponderosa pines, part of the 1.5 million acre Kaibab National Forest. Some of these trees were reported to be 300 to 400 years old.

When I began exploring all the cars, I soon ran into four cowboy musicians and singers who were serenading passengers with Western songs. In another car, I heard an Indian singer, Clarence Clearwater, who was crooning the old Bing Crosby and Andrew Sisters hit, "Along the Navajo Trail." He had also recorded Navajo music which he was selling on CD's.

While there was no commentary on what we were seeing on our journey, a tabloid-sized newspaper with information on the train and a small magazine about the Grand

Historic Grand Canyon Depot.

Canyon were available to everyone.

The altitude at Williams was 6800.' Looking toward the south as we took off, we could see the snow-covered 9,264' Bill Williams Mountain. We crossed Cataract Creek on a 182-foot trestle at mile-post 4 and reached Williams city limits at milepost 5. This was followed by some historic ruins of old supply lines and stations, cattle tanks and abandoned copper mines. Between mileposts 28.5 and 36.7 we viewed the magnificent San Francisco Peaks about thirty miles to the east. These are the highest peaks in Arizona at 12,633' and 12,356'. When we passed Coconino Canyon between mile-posts 54.0 and 58.0, we slowed down to cross several bridges and switchbacks. At 59.9 we entered the National Park, and by 63.7 we had reached the Grand Canyon Station.

We looked for wildlife all along the way as there were supposed to be elk, mule deer, antelope, and rabbits. We only saw a few cows which our hostess, Reeta, called "slow elk." Reeta also said, "If you have questions, don't bother me, I'll be busy!" She had actually retired four years before from the railroad but had been called back on an emergency basis. She was entertaining and kept us all laughing.

Our visit to the Grand Canyon lasted three hours and fifteen minutes and was spectacular. We walked around shooting photos of the magnificent multi-colored canyon from the South Rim. We had learned on the train from an announcement just before arriving that the canyon was 277 river-miles long, an average of ten miles wide and about a mile deep. The Grand

Canyon was declared a National Monument by President Theodore Roosevelt in 1908 and became a federal park in 1919.

After strolling for a while along the rim, my sister and I stopped to browse at Verkamps Curios and the 1905 Hopi House, both large shops carrying museum-quality Indian crafts along with souvenirs. Lunch followed at the historic Bright Angel Lodge (1935) which was situated right next to the rim. Then it was time to return to the train for our ride back to Williams. We departed the log cabin-style Grand Canyon Depot at exactly 1530. As the train got under way with its run back through Coconino Canyon, the gentle rocking of the cars on the rails soon had many passengers snoozing.

Around 1700 the train slowed to a stop and six train robbers jumped on board at the front. It was half-an-hour before these bandits made their way back to our car. With grim faces they sternly demanded our money and jewelry.

Ten minutes later, black-clad Grand Canyon Railway Marshal John B. Goodmore (the "B" stands for "B good or B gone") entered our car and everyone pointed toward the rear where the bandits had gone. Another ten minutes passed and the desperados returned, hands in the air as our hero, the brave Marshal, had successfully rounded them up. We all cheered.

At 1745 the train arrived back in Williams. The sun had already set, and the air was crisp as the large crowd headed back to the Grand Canyon Railway Hotel and into Spenser's Lounge. This relaxing bar and restaurant was named for an artist who had designed the

huge hand-carved 1887 oak wood bar for a pub called the Lion's Den in the small town of Shepard's Bush, England. Other passengers went to Max and Thelma's Restaurant for a hot buffet. It had been a spectacular day of railroading and an unforgettable experience of seeing one of America's most famous tourist destinations, the Grand Canyon National Park.

An autum excursion through the Arizona high desert and canyons on the Verde Canyon Railroad.

CHAPTER TWENTY

ARIZONA VERDE CANYON RAILROAD
November 2004

Diesel locomotive #1512 prepares to pull passengers through Verde Canyon.

CLARKDALE, ARIZONA — The Verde Canyon in late autumn was a riot of color when I viewed it from a window of the first-class car, "Sedona," on the Verde Canyon Railroad. Glimmering yellow-and-gold leaves of cottonwood, sycamores, willows and oak trees shimmered in the bright sun. Green creosote bushes, manzanita and saltbush contrasted colorfully against red sandstone cliffs in a wilderness area untouched by freeways or strip malls.

My husband and I had purchased tickets to ride this tourist railroad from Clarkdale, Arizona north to a ghost town called Perkinsville, a round trip excursion of around four hours representing hundreds of years of Western history. It was the "Old West" at its finest. In fact, I could have been traveling a hundred years ago and ninety-five percent would have looked exactly the same.

Railroading in this northern area of Arizona began in 1895 when a narrow gauge line named the United Verde and Pacific Railroad was opened to haul copper ore from Jerome to Jerome Junction in Chino Valley over 26 miles of tracks. The little railroad then joined the standard gauge

Santa Fe, Prescott and Phoenix.

Built by Montana Senator William Andrews Clark (1839-1925), who had acquired the United Verde Copper Company in 1888, the narrow gauge line operated until 1920.

A fire in the United Verde mine in 1894, which burned for twenty years, forced a new surface plant to be built along with three new standard-gauge railroads and a company town called Clarkdale. The Verde Valley Railroad, one of the three, was financed by Senator Clark but owned by the Santa Fe, Prescott and Phoenix Railroad. It ran 38 miles from Cedar Glade (renamed Drake) to Clarkdale along the Verde River, through Verde and Sycamore Canyons and a man-made tunnel.

In 1953 the Clarkdale smelter was closed and the railroad began hauling cement mined in Clarkdale by the American Cement Company for the construction of the Glen Canyon Dam near Page, Arizona.

Dave and Linda Durbano purchased the Verde Valley from the Santa Fe Railroad in 1988. Mr. Durbano had never actually ridden on the historic line but was impressed by its financial records as a freight-carrier. When he did take his first excursion, he was so awestruck by the overpowering beauty of the wild Arizona cliffs and canyons that he decided to open a tourist railroad.

Excursions began for 160 passengers riding in two coach cars, two open-air cars and one first-class car plus a caboose, pulled by one diesel engine, on November 23, 1990. By 2003, 380 passengers could be counted on each trip using three coaches and five first-class cars. By 2004, the train was carrying six first-class cars, two coaches and a caboose plus five open-air viewing cars. In 1997 a new depot opened with a restaurant, souvenir shop and museum.

Our journey began with a backward view of the old mining town of Jerome, 2000' above the valley floor at 5400' on Mingus Mountain. The Black Hills surrounding Jerome were made up of Mingus Mountain, Cleopatra Hill and Woodchute Mountain. It was here that the copper miners had lived.

Within minutes I had dashed outside from my first class com-

First class passenger car interior

Bar in passenger car of Verde Canyon Railroad.

The Verde Canyon Railroad pulls passengers around a long curve.

partment to an open-air car to begin photographing the scenery, but what we passed through first were the remnants of fifty tons of slag heaps, waste from the old smelter. A tape that began playing informed us that the slag covered an area of 40 acres and was 40' high. Pieces of metal which had once kept the waste material from covering the tracks were rusted and falling apart.

The tape continued and we learned the train would be traveling at a speed of ten-to-twelve miles per hour from mileposts 38 to 18, a distance of twenty miles from Clarkdale to Perkinsville and twenty miles back.

Soon after passing through the slag heap near milepost 38 we saw the Verde River below us on the right, muddy from recent rains.

The river, we learned, was 160 miles long and fed by five major creeks. On our left were Sinagua Indian ruins in the form of caves high up along the cliffs. These were Pre-Colombian people who lived in the Verde Valley between AD 1100 and 1125, displacing a Hohokam tribe. The Sinagua also built masonry structures, some of which can be viewed in nearby Tuzigoot National Monument.

The train ran over the S.O.B. Trestle which traversed a small box canyon. Cliffs on the far side of the winding Verde River provided shelter and nesting areas for bald eagles. Though we were a month too early in November to see the great birds nesting, we did spot four perched on cliffs or trees along the route. My husband, who is especially good at spotting game,

also saw quail, red-tailed hawks, ducks and signs of beaver and otter. We both spied a great blue heron.

After a while the canyon narrowed and its steep walls were covered in shadow. The shimmering yellow leaves of the cottonwood and willow trees faded in the dark light. The river continued to rush along below us, still muddy from recent storms, and there was ample evidence of trees and shrubs which had been pushed over by rampaging water.

We did not leave the train at Perkinsville, our half-way point, but took photographs of the old Perkins Ranch, once used in the movie *How the West Was Won*. A large printed advertisement announced, "Outdoor Activities - train rides, chuck wagon dinners - call 928-636-5007. Steve Rafter -

Marion Perkins."

An old wooden depot, at one time painted yellow, had deteriorated next to the railroad tracks. It all looked like a movie set. We waited while the train engines were run forward on a side track to connect to the other end of the train to pull us back to Clarkdale.

Three blasts from the train whistle and we were ready to take off. I looked at my watch and it was 1114. We headed back toward Clarkdale over a steel bridge, past more Indian dwellings and through a 680-foot black tunnel which had been blasted through solid rock.

I learned from Ed Williams of Clarkdale, a train attendant who had been riding these rails for nine years, that the two FP7 diesel engines that were pulling us, #1510 and #1512, came from Alaska. They had been built in 1953 by the Electro-Motive Division of General Motors and pulled trains from Whittier to Fairbanks and Anchorage to Fairbanks for seventeen years. Between 1988-1995 they were with the Wyoming-Colorado Railroad and only came to the Verde Valley Railroad in 1996. They were refurbished in the train facilities in Clarkdale and painted by artist Doug Allen in an aqua color with striking portraits of bald eagles with yellow beaks and yellow-and-black eyes. They were the most colorful locomotives I had ever seen.

After our return to Clarkdale I learned about the passenger cars. Mary Bertram, who had come out from New Jersey nine years ago and been with the railroad for eight and-a-half years, took me on a tour. Our train had been made up of six first-class cars and two coach cars. The railroad also had a restored

AC&F caboose which could be rented for private parties of six, but it had not been in use on the day we traveled.

The coach cars, restored Pullman Standard, were built in 1946 and 1947 in Illinois, and used for a commuter line on the New York Central. Two of the first-class Budd Stainless Steel cars were built in 1956 and 1957 in Pennsylvania and ran between Chicago and Los Angeles on the Santa Fe's *El Capitan.* One Budd Stainless Steel car came from the Canadian National.

The first-class cars had tan leather couches facing each other for groups of four on one side of the aisle and single cushioned seats also facing each other on the opposite side. Tables were placed between the seats, but there were no overhead racks for coats or packages. Everyone enjoyed large picture windows. Four of the six first-class cars had built-in bars and all had rest rooms.

The two coach cars seated two people on an upright leather seat on each side of the aisle and had racks above. One had a bar built in the back.

The first-class cars provided food for passengers which consisted of muffins, plates of fruit and cherry crepes and other delicacies. Drinks were offered including Coke, Pepsi, Sprite, tea or coffee plus wine and hard liquor. Every first-class passenger was offered one free drink.

All the cars' interiors had been spruced up by two Sedona artists in 2003. Ann Rhinehart and Richard Drayton painted murals, did stenciling and added faux finishes using acrylic and polyurethane paints while the train was actually in

operation. Their job took from mid-June to the end of September, with the artists working eight hour days, four days a week.

Mary Bertram explained that each car had a theme: "'The Tucson Car,' a coach, has blue Naugahyde seats and is painted with indigenous cacti. On the 'Phoenix Car' there is a big sun, while the 'Wickenburg Car' has a cowboy theme and the 'Sedona Car' features native petroglyphs." Even the restrooms were beautifully decorated.

When we ended our journey back in Clarkdale, we were invited to participate in an outdoor barbecue being put on by the restaurant in the depot. A cowboy singer entertained us. His card read, "Have Guitar Will Travel." Will Adams, "Arizona Cowboy Balladeer and Poet," had worked on the train for ten years before he was replaced by the tape. Now he sang daily for a couple of hours at lunch, and we enjoyed the entertainment almost as much as we had the Verde Canyon Railroad. It was truly a memorable four hours of outstanding railroading though the Old West.

The Verde Canyon Railroad is located at 300 North Broadway, Clarkdale, Arizona, 86324-2302; 800-293-7245; 800-320-0718; 928-639-0010; Fax: 928-639-1653. The train can now carry 346 passengers and had around 100,000 passengers in 2005. In April 2006 Verde Canyon Railroad carried their one-millionth passenger. For schedules and current prices: www.verdecanyonrr.com Email: info@verdecanyonrr.com

CHAPTER TWENTY-ONE

CALIFORNIA NAPA VALLEY WINE TRAIN
April 2000

The "Champagne Vista Dome Car" on the Napa Valley Wine Train.

It took the arrival of out-of-town guests for me to finally ride the Napa Valley Wine Train. A woman friend and her husband from Hattiesburg, Mississippi, were in Northern California on business and stopped to visit for a few days. They were both train buffs, so we headed up to Napa to ride the wine train. The adventure turned out to be great fun.

The Napa Valley Wine Train runs on a standard-gauge track between Napa and St. Helena, California. The excursion takes three hours and covers thirty-six miles of track round trip. It makes two round trips on weekdays and three on weekends.

We arrived at the train station in Napa an hour early to check in as requested. The train station is really quite luxurious, with a large lounge featuring upholstered sofas, several gift shops and a café. While we waited, bartenders passed out free Chardonnay to the passengers.

When we boarded the train, I was impressed by the elegance of the Victorian décor. It looked as though no expense had been spared in refurbishing the 1915 Pullman Carriage cars with fine mahogany paneling and other richly-polished woods, crystal chandeliers, gold velvet swivel chairs, booths, wood tables and brass light fixtures.

There were overhead brass coat-racks, gold velvet curtains, a polished brass rail on the observation platform, and a yellow wool carpet with green-and-red designs. Soft music was piped throughout the entire train.

Our train was being pulled by two ALCO American diesel locomotives, FA4s, built in the 1950s and burning natural gas. We were told steam locomotives are not allowed because of local restrictions.

Our train had nine cars including two dining cars, a deli car, a 1950's glass-topped "Champagne Vista Dome Car," a stainless-steel kitchen with observation windows to view preparation of food, and several restored antique parlor or lounge cars. One lounge featured a bar and piano where guests from the first lunch or dinner seating could enjoy wine and desserts on their return journey.

My husband had joined us and we selected four seats at the very end of a Pullman so we could look out on both sides, plus back through the glass door to the open rear platform.

The train left right on time at

The Napa Valley Wine Train dining car.

Chef in the restaurant kitchen car.

1130 hours, carrying about half of its capacity of 300 passengers. Soon we were experiencing the gentle, rocking motions of rolling over rails as we slowly headed north through picturesque vineyards and past some 27 wineries. It was a gorgeous spring day and the vineyards looked well-tended, row after row of stakes of grapevines which would produce a lush fruit harvest in the fall.

Seeing this scene through my friends' eyes was almost like viewing it for the first time myself. The elegant old wineries, and many new ones, and the seemingly endless vineyards made an intriguing spectacle from the windows of the

Waiting for passengers.

curtains hung at the windows and French chairs were upholstered in floral tapestry.

The tables were covered with white damask tablecloths and decorated with a single purple cymbidium orchid. Reed and Barton silver flatware and lead crystal ware accompanied the British bone china.

A wine glass at each setting noted that the "Wine Train had celebrated its 10th anniversary on September 25, 1999," and had carried one million passengers. This train has probably taken 500,000 vehicles off the roads in the Napa Valley.

Our lunch was delicious, with a good selection including farm-raised salmon, smoked pork, portobello mushrooms a la Pyrenees, Sonoma rack of lamb, and free-range chicken breast stuffed with mushrooms.

Desserts included chocolate torte, fruit crisp or the Wine Train's own ice cream. We all ordered something different and found the meals to be well-prepared and very tasty. Other menus are provided for weekend brunch and dinner.

Napa Valley Wine Train.

We ordered champagne and shortly before noon were brought four plates of *hors d' oeuvres* as part of our lunch. There were two meal seatings and we had picked the second one starting at 1300 for the return trip. At St. Helena, the locomotive was brought around and attached to the back end of the train, and we started rolling back to Napa.

Our dining car, the "Le Gourmet," which seated sixty people, was quite elegant, with wide picture windows and glass etched with grapes and leaves. This particular car had a receding white celestial ceiling so air could come through, giving passengers relief from the heat. Ceiling fans were installed in addition to central air-conditioning. Soft music enhanced the car's ambience. Gold velvet

For current schedules and ticket prices: www.winetrain.com or 800-427-4124. Location: Historic Downtown Napa, 1275 McKinstry Street, Napa, CA 94559.

Larry Galliani, a brakeman from Fort Bragg, informs passengers about the Super Skunk train running through the California redwoods.

CHAPTER TWENTY-TWO

CALIFORNIA
THIS SKUNK HAS A PLEASANT AIR
August 1985

Fort Bragg Train Station.

Fort Bragg RR Museum.

FORT BRAGG, CALIFORNIA — In 1985 residents of this Northern California coastal town celebrated the "California Western Railroad Centennial." Their famous "Skunk Railroad" began operation as a logging train in 1885 and had run continually for a century. Today the trains haul passengers and freight forty miles inland to the tiny town of Willits, using both steam and diesel engines and old railroad cars. Occasionally, for light passenger loads, they run bright yellow "rail buses," which were manufactured by Mack Trucks.

These originally were buses with gasoline engines set on rail wheels. They cost about half the price of a steam locomotive and required only a driver and conductor. The rail buses, which began service in 1925, were nicknamed for their gasoline engines. People used to say, "You can smell 'em before you can see 'em, just like a skunk!" Just as popular are the trains pulled by the 1924 Baldwin steam engine, Old No. 45.

The route of the Skunk Railroad is what makes it unique. The line runs through scenic coastal redwoods, over thirty trestles and bridges and through two deep mountain tunnels. From an elevation of eighty feet at Fort Bragg, the rails climb to a summit of 1,740 feet, then descend into Willits at 1,364 feet.

The railroad follows picturesque Pudding Creek and the sparkling Noyo River past old logging camps, isolated cabins, dense forest groves and apple orchards. In the spring, the woods are full of wildflowers such as lady slippers, purple iris, tiger lilies, rhododendrons and wild azaleas. Blue heron, wild ducks and quail are often seen, with occasional sightings of deer and other wild animals.

The trains run from May through December carrying over 100,000 passengers on full and half-day trips. The trains have a capacity of 836 persons using eleven coaches. Riders can choose a half-day round trip to Northspur from either Fort Bragg or Willits, which is what I did. All trains stop at Northspur for passengers to enjoy refreshments and change trains.

We rolled out of Fort Bragg with whistles blowing. Our train carried around 250 people in eight cars, including one open observation car with standing room only. No one was allowed to go into this car until we had cleared the first tunnel.

Once out of town we passed a cemetery, then followed Pudding Creek on our left. Pussy willows grew thick along the water's edge. The sun came out and a majestic blue heron flew overhead. The plants and trees grew thicker, turning into a forest of second-growth redwoods.

I talked with Larry Galliani, the brakeman, who had worked for the railroad for eleven years. He wore a snappy red vest with white shirt, black pants and cap. A gold chain ran from the buttons on his vest to his pocket.

Larry explained that the land through which we were passing and the railroad were owned by Georgia Pacific, which had purchased both from Boise-Cascade in 1973. Before that, the land and the rail-

The Skunk Train following Pudding Creek. The open observation car in the middle is the most popular for photographers.

Skunk Train steam engine.

road were owned by the Union Lumber Company, which was formed in 1891 from the Fort Bragg Redwood Company and the Noyo Lumber Company.

A long blast from the train whistle alerted us to a station half-a-mile up the track. Then we plunged into the 1,200-foot tunnel, which soon grew pitch black.

Before too long we picked up the Noyo River on our right, which we followed all the way to Northspur. Then we were moving under a tunnel of redwood trees with summer sunshine filtering down and the wind blowing our hair.

It took one hour-and-ten minutes to reach Northspur. Sharp turns provided excellent views of the cars ahead. The route was a smooth ride over rumbling bridges, trestles and endless curves.

We passed Camp Noyo, the Boy Scout Explorer camp, Alpine Station (once a hotel resort), and Camp Mendocino, where 1500 youngsters from San Francisco come to enjoy the woods every summer.

Finally there was the red wooden water tower and then Northspur, elevation 322 feet. We could smell a barbecue being prepared and hear blue jays chattering as the train pulled to a stop.

I thought that this "Redwood Route" established for the original Fort Bragg Railroad had changed little since the first trains ran here in the last century. It was a time when rugged loggers loaded their precious cargo to be taken to the abandoned army post of Fort Bragg and then by ships to the market in San Francisco. I was glad that railroad had been built and even happier it was still running 100 years later for us all to enjoy the beauty of the Northern California redwoods.

For up-to-date information:
www.skunktrain.com
Call: 1-800-866-1690

In August 1996 local Mendocino Coast investors purchased California Western and on December 17, 2003, the railroad was purchased by the Sierra Railroad Company. The Skunk Train is located at Highway One and Laurel Street, Fort Bragg, CA.

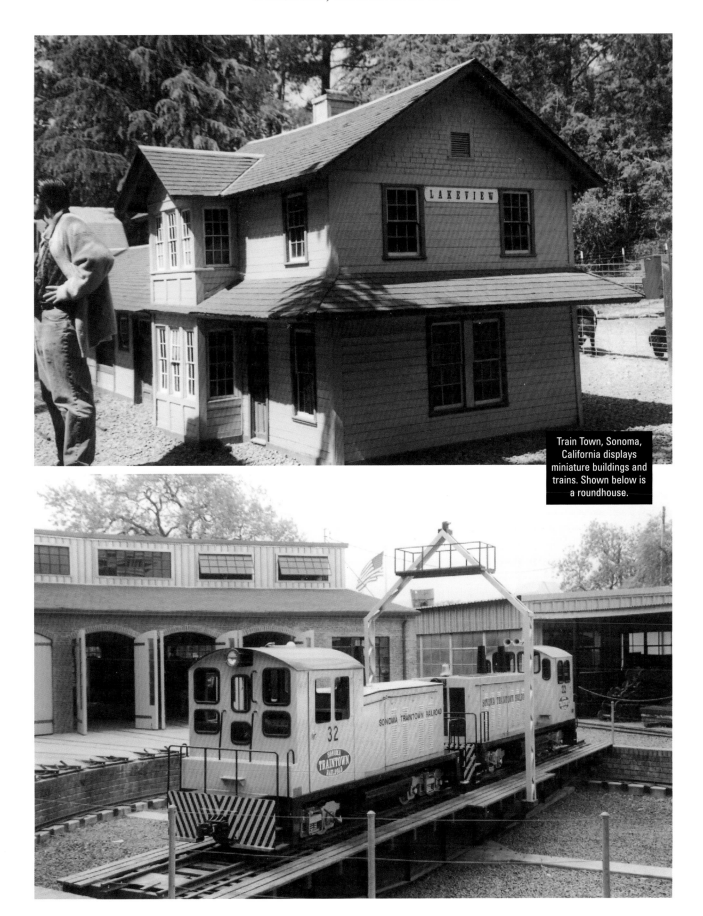

Train Town, Sonoma, California displays miniature buildings and trains. Shown below is a roundhouse.

CHAPTER TWENTY-THREE

CALIFORNIA
A TRAIN FOR THE KIDS
TINY TRAINS RIDE RAILS IN SONOMA
April 2000

Sonoma Train Town RR.

You don't have to be a child to enjoy Train Town in Sonoma, California, since this theme park offers family entertainment for all ages. What started as one man's private hobby, running miniature trains, has developed into a ten-acre railroad park filled with trees, animals, lakes, bridges, tunnels, waterfalls and historic replica structures including three full sized 1930's and 1940's cabooses.

The fifteen-inch gauge tracks carry one-quarter-scale, live steam locomotives and diesel replicas on a ride around the park. The track is one and one-quarter miles long with two tunnels which are 140' and 40' long. In addition, there are five bridges and trestles.

Train Town also has a miniature city and rides including a High Iron Ferris Wheel, Train Town Airlines, the Locomotion, Chattanooga Choo-Choo-Chairs, Iron Horse Carousel and other rides. Visitors will find a petting zoo, snack bar and gift shop.

The big attraction is the miniature railroad which takes passengers on a twenty-minute ride, including a ten-minute stop by an animal corral at Lakeview where the steam locomotive takes on water.

Our train engineer, Thomas Beirden of Sonoma, who restores vintage race cars at Sears Point for a living, said he restored the 2 1/2 ton steam locomotive used to pull the train we rode on. The engine, No

Engineer Beirden drives the ALCO locomotive.

5212, was built in 1937 by a retired engineer for the Alco Company. This locomotive is a Hudson type of the 1930s, an Alco J-la 4-6-4 modeled from the plans of Central No. 5212. At one time the original locomotive pulled the 20th Century Limited on the New York Central Railroad. Beirden said, "When I saw this engine, it reached out to my heart!"

He spent the next three years restoring it, thinking about the time when he would be doing what he is doing now on weekends — driving the seven-car train filled with ninety or so happy people on a track around the park.

Other locomotives at Train Town are steam and gas-run; there is also an electric motor car and a roundhouse. One locomotive is a replica of an 1875 Baldwin Mogel 2-6-0 by Winton Engineering. Another is an SW 1200 1992 custom locomotive.

Train Town is open June 1 through Labor Day from 1000 to 1700 hrs. From September 1

Engineer Thomas Beirden restored this 2 1/2 ton steam locomotive, a 1937 replica of the ALCO which pulled the 20th Century Limited on the New York Central Railroad.

through May, it is open Friday, Saturday and Sundays plus all major holidays except Thanksgiving and Christmas.

The railroad is located one mile south of the Sonoma Town Square at 20264 Broadway (Highway 12), Sonoma, CA. 95476.

For the latest information and fares:
www.traintown.com
Call (707) 938-3912

CHAPTER TWENTY-FOUR

CALIFORNIA
YOSEMITE MOUNTAIN SUGAR PINE RAILROAD
April 2002

1928 twelve-wheel, 82 ton wood-burning Shay locomotive.

On my last visit to Yosemite National Park in Northern California, I was able to take a ride on the Sugar Pine Railroad in the Sierra National Forest just south of the park. Our ride, late in the afternoon, took an hour, followed by a Western steak barbecue and live music. It was a most entertaining evening.

Narrow-gauge railroads were built throughout the Sierras as logging trains. We were told that the equipment on the Sugar Pine Railroad came from the Tuolumne area, which had logging from 1908 to 1924. Actual logging in the whole mountain area ran for close to sixty years beginning in 1874. Pine trees such as ponderosa, sugar pines, cedar trees and white firs were heavily logged with no replanting. Nearly one and-a-half billion board feet of lumber were harvested, and the forests now are all new growth.

The antique steam engine pulling our little train was a twelve-wheel wood-burning Shay, No. 10, built in 1928 for a 36-inch narrow gauge logging operation. The train company, called the "Madera Sugar Pine Lumber Company Railroad," ran from 1899 to 1931. The original Shay engine used for our trip weighed 82 1/2 tons and ran fifteen mph burning oil and pulling four cars of passengers. A section of the original railbed has been reconstructed using the same techniques used at the turn of the century.

Our scenic excursion through quiet pine forests was interrupted with a "robbery" by two masked bandits who came galloping up on horses. They shot pistols and yelled, "This is a hold up!" After examining all the passengers' hats and jewelry, the bandits decided we were not rich enough and returned the items before galloping away.

We stopped again in a picnic area where our Shay steam engine took on water. It needed 400 gallons of water for our four-mile round-trip. In the summer when more than one train runs, people can ride on an early train taking a picnic lunch, then board a later train to return.

By the time the train ride was over and dinner finished, it was quite late, so my husband and I spent the night in Yosemite National Park area in the Clark Cottages, part of "old Yosemite." These cottages were built in 1876 with the main building constructed in 1879.

The Yosemite Mountain Sugar

A "robbery" on the Sugar Pine Railroad.

Pine Railroad operates in the Sierra National Forest, 56001 Yosemite Highway 41, Fish Camp, CA 93623. It operates daily from March through October. Besides the "Logger Steam Train," special runs include a "Moonlight Special," and rides on the trolley-like "Jenny Railcars" powered by antique Model "A" Ford gas engines. These were once used to provide transportation for logging and track repair crews. In addition, there are group excursions, including barbecues and field trips for school children.

For up-to-date information: www.ymsprr.com or call: 1-559-683-7273.

Two vintage Shay steam locomotives have been brought in from the Westside Lumber Company and restored to provide authentic motive power for the train. Number 10, built in 1928, weighs 83 tons and is the heaviest operating narrow-gauge Shay locomotive today.

For information on Yosemite National Park: www.yosemitepark.com

CHAPTER TWENTY-FIVE

CALIFORNIA
SAN FRANCISCO STILL HOOKED ON CABLE CARS
February 1985 - October 2005

San Francisco cable car.

S AN FRANCISCO — It is a summer morning here, typically foggy and cold. Andrew Hallidie, a wire rope manufacturer, is about to make history operating the first cable railway, also known a "Hallidie's Folly." He will go from the top of Nob Hill at Jones Street six blocks down to Clay Street. He has hired the world's first gripman to help him operate his new contraption.

His employee takes one look down the hill through the fog, panics and disappears. Hallidie, confi-

dent that the screw-type grip he has invented will hold his car safely against the underground cable, grabs the grip-wheel and guides the car down a sixteen percent grade at four miles per hour.

The date is August 2, 1873. History has been made.

Hallidie's invention of cars powered by connection to an endless loop of cable marked the beginning of the end of the horse-drawn cars, a trend that spread to major cities throughout the world. By the turn of the century, San Francisco had several companies

operating cable cars.

In the 1880s electric streetcars, found to be more efficient, began to replace the cable cars. Futhermore, in 1906 a major earthquake destroyed most of the network in San Francisco, and only a few lines remained.

After the quake, electric trolley buses began replacing even more cars until only five lines were left in jeopardy of extinction. City officials were in the mood to modernize. Only a last-minute fight by San Francisco citizens led by Freidel Klussmann, who became known as the "Cable Car Lady," saved three of these lines.

Finally, in 1955 a city charter guaranteed maintenance and perpetuation of these three existing cable car lines. The cable car system was also declared a special "moving" National Historic Landmark by the National Park Service on October 1, 1964.

Meanwhile, through the years the cable cars continued to operate carrying shoppers, school children, business people, and tourists up and down the hills of San Francisco. A few minor improvements were made, such as the installation of electric windshield wipers, a slight change in the grip design, and brighter headlights.

Residents lived with the sound of clanging bells, the squeal of tourists heading down steep hills, and the banter of the conductors and gripmen. The cable cars became San Francisco's top tourist attraction.

In 1979 the system rattled to a halt, the victim of more than one hundred years of wear and tear. Emergency repairs were made, but reports stressed the need of a major overhaul.

A massive "Save the Cable Car Campaign" was launched under the leadership of Mayor Dianne Feinstein (now a United States Senator from California). Ten miles of new track was laid, the cars repaired, and a new cable car barn erected over a period of twenty months between September 21,1982 and June 21, 1984. It was a $60 million renovation.

Today the cable cars are back carrying capacity crowds throughout the city. A good way to learn about them is to visit the Cable Car Museum located in the Cable Car Barn and Powerhouse.

The brick walls of this structure, erected after the 1906 earthquake, were cracked and sagging. During the renovation project, the walls were reinforced with thousands of pounds of Gunite, and the windows were shored up with epoxy.

On exhibit at the museum are old wooden cars from the Sutter Street Railway, a replica of an antique Market Street car, sixteen wooden models of cars, old photos, a bell you can ring and a gift shop.

Visitors may view the machinery that runs the San Francisco cable cars. It is extremely noisy. A sign explains: "San Francisco cable cars have no motors of their own. They are towed along tracks in the street by a moving cable. This is the only operating cable car system in the world."

The cables move at 9 1/2 miles per hour; there are 44 cable cars in the system, and 27 operate at one time. The single-ended cars operate on Powell, Mason and Hyde. The double-ended cars run on California St., but may also operate on Powell, Mason and Hyde. The single-ended cars are turned on a turntable when they reach the end of the line.

In the "Sheave Room" downstairs, visitors can see "where all four cables enter and exit the power house." A sign continues: "They arrive here from all directions and are turned on wheels (sheaves) to align with the cable machinery…Look closely and you can see the cables pass directly below you."

All three cable car routes begin or end on Market Street, a major restored thoroughfare that slashes through the city in a northeast-southwest direction. They pass the major sightseeing areas of the city including Union Square, Nob Hill, Chinatown, the Cable Car Barn and Museum, Russian Hill, Lombard Street (famous crooked street), and Fisherman's Wharf.

And when you are riding a cable car down those steep San Francisco streets with the wind blowing your hair and the bell ringing, you will know you have arrived and are enjoying one of the most beautiful and unique cities in the world. Hang on to your hat!

For up-to-date information:
www.sfcablecar.com

www.sfcablecar.com/history.html
www.cablecarmuseum.org
www.sfmuni.com - (Link to MUNI)

Inside the historic Cable Car Barn & Powerhouse, located at 1201 Mason St. (corner of Mason and Washington Sts.) which is free to visitors, you can watch the actual cable winding machinery and mechanical devices such as grips, track cable and brake mechanisms. On display are three antique cable cars and a photo narration of the reconstruction of the system from 1982-1984. Open every day except Thanksgiving, Christmas and New Year's Day.

CHAPTER TWENTY-SIX

COLORADO
RIDE THE NARROW GAUGE FROM DURANGO TO SILVERTON
July 1984 - July 1985 - July 1986

The Durango and Silverton Narrow Gauge train in Silverton, Colorado.

SILVERTON, COLORADO — Gold, that precious glittering commodity for which men have cheerfully killed, was discovered in the San Juan Mountains of Colorado, specifically in Arasta Gulch, by a party sponsored by Governor Pike of New Mexico in 1870.

By 1874 the gold rush was on. It had been in full force in California between 1848 and 1858. Now prospectors hurried to this remote Colorado area with dreams of buckets of gold, and many of

their dreams came true. More than a billion dollars in metal ores, gold and silver, have gone through Silverton in the past 100 years.

The wealth was found in Arasta Gulch, in Kendall and Sutton Mountains, and in gulches with name like Maggie and Minnie, Cunningham, Eureka, Placer and Poughkeepsie, plus Mineral Point and Red Mountain.

The gold was there for the taking if one could figure a way to get it out. Pack horses and mules were used, wagon roads built when pos-

sible, even aerial tramways. Then someone thought to build a narrow-gauge railroad.

The construction of the Denver and Rio Grande Railway branch line from Durango into Silverton was completed in July 1882. This greatly reduced the cost of transporting the gold and silver from the 1876 price of $60 a ton for pack train service, to $12 a ton in 1882.

Today, the only Denver and Rio Grande branch line that remains open is the 45-mile run between Durango and Silverton. Today it hauls tourists who have a nostalgia for railroads or just want the pleasure and excitement of this scenic ride.

Owner Charles E. Bradshaw Jr. renamed the line the Durango and Silverton Narrow Gauge Railroad Co., added new runs, refurbished old railroad engines from the 1920s, and coaches, many of which were from the 1880s. He added open gondola cars and set up a bus-train combination between the two cities.

The *Durango and Silverton Narrow Gauge* claims to be the only regularly scheduled and regulated steam-powered, 100 percent coal-fired, narrow-gauge railroad in the United States. It provides several runs a day which take three hours each way. Passengers are also pro-

vided with a couple of hours to explore the town of Silverton.

On the day I traveled I started from Silverton. The train was made up of a black steam-puffing engine and seven yellow cars consisting of coaches and open gondola cars plus a concessionaire car selling drinks, food and souvenirs. For the best view I had been advised to sit on the left going down from this old silver city.

It was a crisp, bright day early in July when we pulled out from Blair Street in Silverton with a couple of hard lurches. The whistle blew, and we found ourselves chugging and swaying past the antique yellow train station, a sand and gravel works, two rushing waterfalls and over what I learned was Mineral Creek.

The brakeman, wearing blue

overalls and a railroad cap, came to collect our tickets about the time our route joined the swollen Animas River. Although signs forbid it, people hung way out over the railings taking photos. Others had already gone to sleep.

I looked back at Silverton and the high mountains surrounding it. Many were still covered with patches of snow glistening in the sun. In the next three hours we would pass over forty-five miles of track, through Animas Canyon and the two-million-acre San Juan National Forest, and past old mine pits and abandoned shacks, decreasing our altitude from 9,318 feet at Silverton to 6,512 feet in Durango.

We crossed and continued to follow the Animas River. Waterfalls plunged down on the west side of the steep gorge. Purple wildflowers

The *Durango and Silverton Narrow Gauge* steams over the "High Line" through the San Juan Mountains of Colorado.

The Animas River.

grew along the banks.

A girl entered our car and announced that beer and wine were for sale in the concession car and added that the drinking age in Colorado is 21. I found out later that these beverages are only available on the afternoon run.

I felt a heavy vibration in the car although the tracks seems pretty solid. From my vantage point I could get lovely views of the train in front as the engine pulled the cars around the curves following the rushing river.

The open gondola cars were yellow wood with brown leather seats facing out. A central aisle ran between them. The roofs were particle board covered with aluminum-colored paint. The trim and iron bars were black, as was the

lantern and wheel in the back car.

There continued to be steep cliffs on either side of the river and more waterfalls flowing down over the rocks. We passed an old water tank on the left and Kendall Creek running swiftly into the river. Signs labeled old abandoned mines.

The train crossed the river and the rock walls became very close to the cars on the left or east side. We could smell the smoke and steam from the engine as the train continued to lurch and rattle around the curves. We passed a bridge and the Grenadier River.

The tracks then ran through Elk Park at an elevation of 8,883 feet, a lovely green meadow bright with spring flowers. There were yellow dandelions, red Indian paintbrush, primroses and purple lupine.

I looked in vain for deer, knowing they are plentiful in these mountains.

The Animas River became wide and meandering in this area, with islands in the middle covered with logs and driftwood. Hundreds of new rail ties, well-oiled and stacked along the track, were ready for some repair work.

We chugged by white aspen forests and fir trees, an old railroad bridge and evidence of landslides. Then we crossed Elk Creek and passed over the Animas River on a 222-foot steel girder bridge. The water below us was white and foamy.

The river was now on our right, its turbulent waters rushing over heavy boulders. There was evidence of more slides. I could smell the smoke from the engine, now quite heavy, and asked a couple next to me if there was much difference in the ride going up than in coming down. They replied that it felt the same except that there was much more smoke and soot blowing back on the climb up as more coal was needed for the engine. The sky seemed suddenly filled with black smoke. I could literally smell the fire.

I decided to walk ahead two cars to the concession car where I bought a drink and a blue-and-white striped train cap labeled "Durango and Silverton Narrow Gauge." The car had a high counter and shelves to carry supplies to guest ranches, plus other gear needed by the nearly 200 hikers and backpackers the train carries every week. There were no tables and chairs in the car although there is one parlor car, called the "Alamosa," which has been rebuilt with an interior of ash wood, a fancy bar, and seats with tables for 28 adults. This car is the last one on the train in summer. It is also added to one of the trains that go as far as Cascade Canyon in the winter.

The coach cars had twelve rows of seats with four seats across or two people on each side with an aisle in the middle. All faced forward. Some were upholstered in what looked like brown leather and others were a green plastic. A touch of elegance was added by lovely oak or birch paneling on the walls and shiny brass doorknobs. Restrooms were at the end of the coach cars.

We continued through forests of aspen, birch and fir trees. High jagged mountain peaks stretched up in the distance. There was another low footbridge, more

slides, a wrecked railroad bridge and a shaky foot bridge used by fishermen and backpackers. Just beyond the Tefft milepost was a sawmill once operated at an elevation of 7,712 feet. Spruce trees were cut here for railroad ties and timber used in the mines.

We slowed down to cross the Animas River on a steel span and shortly after entered Cascade Canyon, where a wye was constructed in 1891 for turning the trains around.

Cascade Canyon has been used in several films, including scenes from the 1949 *Ticket to Tomahawk* with Dan Dailey, *Around the World in Eighty Days*, with David Niven, and *Night Passage*, with Jimmy Stewart and Audie Murphy.

We passed a new lodge being built and made a stop at Tall Timber Resort, which was also used for movies. Scenes from *Butch Cassidy and the Sundance Kid* with Robert Redford and Paul Newman were shot here. This was followed by Silver Falls on the east side cascading down a cliff, then a red miniature mail coach, cabins, horses, mules and various trails leading off into the wilderness. Next came the red brick Tacoma power plant in use since 1905, Crazy Woman Creek, and a big steel bridge across the river. The canyon was filled with smoke.

Finally, we entered the most spectacular part of the three-hour trip as the train inched slowly up, and then along the High Line, a narrow shelf 400 feet above the river. This was a very scary precipice. The water was far below, and the train wheels only inches from the edge of the cliff. It was hard to see and when we did get a glimpse of the river, it appeared

foaming white and green.

We passed between five short cuts through the hard red granite, then two long ones. The last, called the Rockwood Cut, is 120 feet long, and was used in *Around the World in Eighty Days* disguised as a tunnel.

The train rocked and swayed… cha CHUG, cha CHUG, squeak, clunk, cha CHUG. Our bodies swayed in an endless rhythm. We passed a raft on the river and the occupants waved, as did some young people riding horses near the tracks.

We continued on into Durango, our spectacular adventure over.

The regular train season with runs between Durango and Silverton is roughly from May through October. The winter trains travel as far as Cascade Canyon. The railroad currently lists ten steam locomotives on their equipment roster. The three steam locomotives are #473, a K-28 bulit in 1923; #478, a K-28 also built in 1923; and a #486, a K-36 built in 1925.

For up-to-date ticket and other information: www.durangotrain.com

The Durango and Silverton Narrow Gauge Railroad Co. is located at 479 Main Ave., Durango, Colorado 81301, 970-247-2733. Toll free:1- 877-872-4607; For Durango Tourism: 1-800-463-8726.

CHAPTER TWENTY-SEVEN

FLORIDA
DISNEY WORLD'S VINTAGE TRAIN LOCOMOTIVES
October 1986

The entrance to Disney World, Orlando.

ORLANDO, FLORIDA — The locomotive builds up steam as passengers prepare to board the Disney World Train. We are in a well-appointed waiting-room in the Main Street Station with gold-and-brown marble floors, cream-colored walls, extensive wood trim and white glass ball chandeliers.

At last the conductor is ready, and excited passengers hurry through double glass doors to climb into open passenger cars decorated with red striped awnings. The train moves slowly out, the steam whistle blows, and we are on our way.

There are four authentic steam locomotives now pulling passenger trains at Disney World in Orlando, Florida. The 1.4 mile ride takes patrons from the Main Street Station past Adventureland, through a tunnel and into Frontierland, where a stop is made to pick up passengers.

The route then passes Thunder Mountain Railroad where prospectors are panning for gold along streams. The train crosses a bridge over water, passes an Indian camp with teepees, then races by several elk. The whistle blows a long, two short and one long shrill sounds. Hissing steam escapes.

Fantasyland becomes evident when passengers can view the top of Cinderella's Castle. This is followed by Tomorrowland and Space Mountain. Disney's famous contemporary hotel can be seen on the left and the Carousel of Progress appears on the right.

After passing the monorail station, the train arrives back at the Main Street Station completing a twenty minute run.

The engines, all built at the Baldwin Locomotive works in Philadelphia, originally were contracted for use in the Yucatan area of Mexico by the Meridian Railways. Walt Disney purchased them for Disney World and had them restored by the Dixon Boiler Works in the Tampa Shipyards of Florida in the late 1960s and early 70s. George Britton, in charge of the restoration project, was then hired by Disney to handle the maintenance of the trains for Disney World.

The four Baldwin locomotives include the "Walter E. Disney," now painted a bright shiny red and restored in 1971. It has a wheel arrangement of 4-6-0 and track leverage of 45,000 pounds, about the same as the other three.

The others are called the "Roy," named for Walt's brother and originally built in 1916; the "Lilly Belle," honoring Walt's wife,

built in 1928; and finally the 1925 "Roger," named for Walt's good friend, Roger A. Broggie, who built a personal railroad for Disney around his home in California.

When the 36" gauge locomotives were restored, they were converted from wood and coal to oil-burning. Conductor Don Fisher explained that wood is difficult to obtain, and two or three tons of coal were needed to burn every hour.

Although all four trains are in good running order, only two are operated at a time. Each can carry 375 to 400 passengers. The charge for riding any of the trains is included in the cost of admission to Disney World.

For the latest information:
http://disneyworld.disney.go.com

A paragraph on this internet site says, "Walt Disney was a great train aficionado. He had a train, the Carolwood Pacific Railroad, in the backyard of his California home. His wife Lillian didn't object to Walt building a railroad in their backyard as long as he didn't disturb her flower garden. Walt built a tunnel so the trains wouldn't disturb her roses." And the rest is history.
Also on the website is news of a special train tour: "Disney's the Magic Behind Our Steam Trains Tour — Venture into the Magic Kingdom before the Park opens, and accompany the railroad engineers as they ready the massive steam trains for another day of service. Walk the backstage roundhouse where the trains are stored and serviced, and ride the rails as you explore how Walt Disney's lifetime love of steam trains led to their becoming an integral part of the Magic Kingdom.
All Aboard!"

A restored Baldwin locomotive named for Walt Disney.

CHAPTER TWENTY-EIGHT

HAWAII
THE SUGAR CANE TRAIN
June 1986

The Lahaina, Kaanapali and Pacific RR, Maui, Hawaii.

MAUI, HAWAII — The Lahaina, Kaanapali and Pacific Rail Road, also known as the Sugar Cane Train, runs from the old whaling village of Lahaina, past the fashionable resort area of Kaanapali, to Puukolii, a distance of around six miles.

The trip takes a half-hour one way traveling at fifteen miles per hour and provides spectacular views of the Pacific Ocean, the channels between Maui and the islands of Molokai and Lanai, and the mountains rising up from the sea.

The route follows the highway, turns up through the sugar cane fields, stops for passengers at the Kaanapali golf course, then parallels the highway again until reaching the boarding platform at Puukolii. During the winter months, whales are seen breaching out of the channel waters.

The conductor sings to the passengers, then launches into colorful stories about the sugar cane and the train. He told us that the *Lahaina, Kaanapali and Pacific Rail Road* is an authentic replica of an old Hawaiian sugar cane railroad that ran in 1890. The open air coaches, now built of steel and fiberglass, are patterned after the old wooden Kalakauan cars that ran on Maui and the Big Island of Hawaii around the turn of the century.

While the original coaches were smaller, the wooden seats facing forward incorporating iron grill

The Lahaina, Kaanapali and Pacific Rail Road Station. Maui, Hawaii.

work with the initials L & K and a whale, are the same. Each coach can carry fifty people.

The 36-inch gauge steam engines used to pull the train were built in 1943 by the H.K. Porter Co. for the Carbon Limestone Co. of Pennsylvania. It was during World War II, and diesel engines could not be produced because of the shortage of copper. After the war, the steam engines were abandoned and sat around until 1968 when they were purchased by A.W. "Mac" McKelvy who was in the rebuilding business. He sold them to the company that was constructing the Sugar Cane Train in Maui. In 1969 A.W. McKelvy got together with the Makai Corporation and created the Lahaina Kaanapali Railroad. The line has operated passenger service from Lahaina to Puukolii (just north of Kaanapali)

daily for more than thirty-five years. Since 1970, over five million tourists to Maui have ridden the train, making it one of West Maui's most popular attractions.

The original Pioneer Mill Railroad line, which was only thirty inches wide, hauled sugar cane to the mills and transported workers between the cane fields and the plantation villages. The railroad line was torn up in 1952 and rebuilt. The two Porter engines, both with 2-4-0 wheel alignments, were cosmetically changed on the outside to appear like the old Hawaiian engines. They were painted a bright blue with a black boiler.

To accommodate passengers, the trains are met at the Lahaina station by double-decker British buses which transport people to downtown Front St. in Lahaina,

the historic Baldwin House, the whaling ship, old prison and the main shopping centers.

Gary Getman, general manager of the railroad, said the train carries 200,000 passengers annually. "We take ten trips a day, 363 days a year (closed Thanksgiving and Christmas)."

For up-to-date information:
www.sugarcanetrain.com

According to this internet site, the trains run thirteen trips a day plus a Dinner Train on Thursday evenings and is now open on Thanksgiving.
The Lahaina Kaanapali Railroad is located at 975 Limahana Pl. Suite #203, Lahaina, Maui, HI 96761. Phone: (808) 667-6851 or toll free: 1-800-499-2307.

CHAPTER TWENTY-NINE

NEW HAMPSHIRE
A CHRISTMAS RUN ON THE POLAR EXPRESS
CONWAY SCENIC RAILROAD
July 1996

The Conway Scenic Railroad awaits passengers at its station in North Conway, New Hampshire.

NORTH CONWAY, NEW HAMPSHIRE — A young boy lays quietly in bed on Christmas eve waiting for Santa. He hears the ringing bells of a sleigh. His friends have told him there is no Santa, but he knows they are wrong. Years later the boy, as a man, remembers: "Late that night I did hear sounds, though not of ringing bells. From outside came the sounds of hissing steam and squeaking metal. I looked through my window and saw a train standing perfectly still in front of my house."

Thus begins Chris Van Allsburg's delightful tale of *THE POLAR EXPRESS* (published by Houghton Mifflin Co., Boston, 1985), which is now being reenacted by the "Believe In Books Literary Foundation" which has an arrangement with the Conway Scenic Railroad in New Hampshire.

The book continues: "'All aboard,' the conductor cried. I ran up to him.

'Well,' he said, 'are you coming?'

'Where?' I asked.

'Why, to the North Pole of course,' was his answer. 'This is the *Polar Express*.' I took his outstretched hand and he pulled me aboard."

Today this scene is being reenacted with space for 5,000 passengers in the month of December to visit the "North Pole." The Conway Scenic Railroad *Polar Express* began in 1995 with five runs and was such a success the schedule has been expanded to twelve. As in the book, the train is filled with children, many in pajamas and nightgowns, who sing Christmas carols, drink chocolate and eat candies.

Russ G. Seybold, the enthusiastic president of this tourist railroad, explained how the idea for the *Polar Express* developed and how popular it proved to be the first time they tried it:

"There were 400 people on each train. When we reached the 'North Pole,' sixty costumed elves carrying lanterns came out to greet the children. The youngsters, all wildly excited, were divided into groups of eight to ten and taken inside where a man dressed in yellow pajamas and a purple robe read Chris Van Allsburg's book. We did a complete recreation of the story in which Santa arrives in his sleigh and picks one child to sit on his knee. The child can request any present he desires."

The boy in Van Allsburg's story wanted a silver bell from Santa's sleigh. Santa gave it to him, but the boy had a hole in his pocket and lost it. At the end of the book, Santa gives him a new bell for Christmas.

Passenger car
"Mount Washington".

In the New Hampshire reenactment, the children are all given hot chocolate and candies. On the ride back in the train they are presented with bells, one each attached to a rawhide thong.

While the *Polar Express* may be its most popular run, the Conway Scenic Railroad operates regularly-scheduled trains from mid-April through late December, using both steam and diesel/electric locomotives. There are two valley routes between North Conway and Conway and North Conway and Bartlett. The first runs 11 miles roundtrip through the Mt. Washington Valley and the surrounding White Mountains and takes 55 minutes. The second runs 21 miles roundtrip to Bartlett and back and takes one and three-quarters hours.

A third route takes passengers through the fabled Crawford Notch, which offers sheer bluffs, steep ravines, cascading streams, the tall Frankenstein Trestle (75' high and 500' long) and the Willey Brook Bridge (95' high from the river and 120' long.) This roundtrip is 50 miles and takes five and one-half hours with the train traveling an average of 15 to 20 MPH (24 to 32 kph).

A luncheon run on the valley route takes an hour and three-quarters, and a dinner trip, with food provided, two hours.

I tried the Sunset dinner run and was impressed with the elegant setting in the Chocorua Dining Car. The entrees included grilled rack of pork, grilled Atlantic salmon and pasta with sun-dried tomatoes. Everyone ordered something different and all proved to be delicious choices.

After dining we enjoyed sitting in the beautifully-restored 1898 Pullman parlor-observation car, "Gertrude Emma." This car offered a rich mahogany interior, large picture windows that opened and individual wicker chairs.

Also of interest were the model railroads run by the North Conway Model Railroad Club. An exhibit is open in the summer in the Freight House adjacent to the North Conway Railroad Station.

For up-to-date information:
www.polarexpress.org
Direct link for the "Polar Express" train.

In 2004 a film based on the book was released by Warner Brothers starring Tom Hanks.
For information on the railroad:
www.conwayscenic.com

CHAPTER THIRTY

NEW HAMPSHIRE
THE RAILWAY TO THE MOON
THE MOUNT WASHINGTON COG RAILWAY
July 1996

A single cog wheel engine ready to push a passenger car up Mount Washington waits at the base station for passengers to finish loading.

MOUNT WASHINGTON COG RY.

B RETTON WOODS, NEW HAMPSHIRE — The day I boarded the Mt. Washington Cog Railway was rare indeed. The sun was shining, there were lovely blue skies, and the wind was light until we got to the very top, and even then not too fierce.

I sat in the first seat on the right with an open window offering a gorgeous view of the mountain. Our passenger car was being pushed by a single cogwheel engine driven by steam, a system that had been put into operation some 135 years earlier. The man who invented it was Sylvester Marsh, and he was ridiculed at the time for trying to build a railroad to the moon. Mount Washington is the highest peak in the Northeastern United States.

My railroad car had wooden walls and a rounded wooden ceiling. The seats were made of metal painted green with green plastic upholstery. I counted fourteen rows which were staggered down so the top row was around fourteen feet higher than the lowest. Four people could be tightly seated in each row, designed with level seats.

A platform beyond my window allowed the passengers to stand outside and take photos of the spectacular scenery. The average wind velocity usually experienced by passengers standing on this platform was 37 mph (60 kmh) but Mt. Washington also holds the world's record of 231 mph (370 kmh) recorded in April 1934. A man fixing something on a roof of a building at the top of the mountain actually recorded this and lived to tell the tale.

There are no switchbacks on Mt. Washington like the famous historic Mt. Tamalpais "Crookedest Railroad in the World" in

Northern California. This track just goes three miles straight up to an altitude of 6288' with an average climb of 25%. This increases to an incredible 37% on a grade called "Jacob's Ladder."

The cog railway is powered by a roaring two-thousand degree fire which burns a ton of coal on each trip to the summit in addition to drinking in 1,000 gallons of water.

This makes for a lot of smoke and soot which delights some passengers and causes others to fret, especially those wearing white. Chunks of coal can be seen scattered all the way up, and I saw several wooden ties burning along the track. Train personnel carry water to squirt on these fires.

Halfway up there are switches where trains can be put on sidings to allow others to pass. These were put in by Henry Teague, who owned the cog railroad from 1931-51. In the summer there are six or seven trains running up and down the mountain daily; passengers can see and photograph each other.

The tracks are all built on a raised wooden trestle which varies in height from one foot to 40' in height. The power comes from the traction on the inside track provided by a toothed cog gear. The outside rails are just guides.

Some ties appeared to me to be missing while others were quite crooked, but we inched our way up safely at four mph shaking and rattling noisily all the way. I learned later that our car had a separate set of brakes from the steam engine, a good safety feature.

The scenery on our sunny day was just spectacular with views into other New England states and Canada. We passed through three alpine zones which included forests

Heavy smoke pours from the Washington Cog Railway engine as it ascends a three mile grade called "Jacobs Ladder."

at the bottom with stunted trees because of heavy winds, a middle section which we were told compares to Labrador, and the top which is tundra with fifteen feet to twenty feet of permafrost.

At the top we toured some historic buildings, plus the modern Sherman Adams Observation Center which contained a museum, restaurant, gift shop and rest rooms.

The train excursion takes three hours round trip which includes a twenty-minute stop at the summit. We came down in a van on a road that runs from the top. Part of the road was purposefully dirt to slow down the vehicle drivers. Many hikers crossed in front of us on the famous Appalachian Trail.

We stayed at the grand old Mount Washington Hotel built in

1902 and owned by the same people who own the cog railway. The hotel was beautifully restored with long white verandas and a red roof. The food was outstanding and other activities were available such as golf, tennis, horseback riding, hiking and swimming.

For up-to-date information and reservations: www.thecog.com.

Call 1-800-922-8825. In New Hampshire: 603-278-5404 The train runs roughly from May through November with a ski train operating in the winter.

www.mtwashington.com
The Mount Washington Hotel

CHAPTER THIRTY-ONE

NEW MEXICO - COLORADO
CUMBRES AND TOLTEC SCENIC RAILROAD
September 1985

Baldwin engine 484 nears a water tank on the Cumbres and Toltec Railroad.

CHAMA, NEW MEXICO — The conductor holds up his walkie-talkie, flips a switch and cries, "Highball it!" Our narrow-gauge steam train pulled by 1925 Baldwin engine No. 484 on the *San Juan Express*, pulls boldly out and our adventure aboard the Cumbres and Toltec Scenic Railroad has begun.

For the rest of the day we will journey back through more than 125 years of Western history. Our course will take us east over one of the most scenic routes in the world, the high country of New Mexico and Colorado.

The enginemen will drive fearlessly over 10,000 foot mountain passes, through vast valleys and blossoming alpine meadows. Before the day is over we will be astonished by the strange giant rock formations near Phantom Curve, and by the breathtaking Toltec Gorge which drops 600 feet below our wheels. We will be captivated by the beauty of the snow-capped San Juan Mountains, the crystal-clear rivers and dazzling white aspen forests.

The track runs 64 miles between Chama, New Mexico and Antonito, Colorado. It was once part of the vast narrow-gauge empire of the Denver and Rio Grande Railroad, built to serve rich mining camps.

Our enginemen were Russ Fischer and Earl Knobb, and the conductor, Greg Stabolepszy. The brakeman was a woman, the first on this railroad, Marty Fischer of Chama.

The seats were hard plastic chairs bolted to the wooden floor of a former boxcar. The sides of the car had been cut out and fitted with squares of plastic serving as windows which could be lowered in warm weather. The rest was authentic 1903 boxcar crude.

Our route took us east from Chama, elevation 7,863, across the Chama River and the Lobato Trestle, into Colorado and up a four percent grade to the Cumbres Summit at 10,015 feet.

Passing lovely fields of wild-flowers, we continued to Windy Point, with gorgeous views of Wolf Creek and the Chama Valley, and then we crossed a wooden trestle over State Highway 17. Next came Tanglefoot Curve where the rails climbed up 39 feet in a long, single loop, and Los Pinos Water Tank, elevation 9,710 feet.

We crossed the river on a 175-foot pile trestle and enjoyed views of an enchanting tree-covered valley. After the Cascade Trestle, 409 feet long and 137 feet high, we rolled into Osier, Colorado.

Osier, meaning "willow," has been the spot for the lunch break since 1885. Passengers used to pay 75 cents and were expected to eat in twenty minutes. Now a cooked lunch is included in the price of the ticket, and we had an hour.

After eating we continued east into New Mexico and up along jagged cliffs. It began to rain as our little train plunged into the blackness of the famous "Rock," or "Toltec" tunnel. Blasted through solid rock, the tunnel curved 360 feet through the mountain. We emerged into a foggy world of strange shapes, pedestals of rocks

Baldwin engine 489 stops to give passenges a lunch break in Osier, Colorado.

sticking up like weird gigantic statues.

Back into Colorado we went through Calico Cut and past Phantom Curve, so named by trainmen who have seen strange ghostly silhouettes among the rocks reflected from the lights of their trains. Far below, Toltec Creek snaked along the bottom of a steep gorge.

We returned to New Mexico and rolled quickly through the 349-foot Mud Tunnel. There were shimmering forests of quaking aspen trees in this area, and views of a valley called "Canada Jarosita."

We then arrived at Big Horn Wye, elevation 9,022 feet. Our ride through the mountains had ranged in elevation from 7863' to 10,015'.

The final part of the route to Antonito ran about eighteen more miles crossing the New Mexico/Colorado border several more times and decreasing in elevation to 7,888 feet.

I felt sad when the ride was over. The Cumbres and Toltec

steam train had provided me with one of the most unforgettable railroading adventures I had ever experienced.

The Cumbres and Toltec Scenic Railroad, America's highest and longest narrow gauge railway, is owned by the states of Colorado and New Mexico and operates daily (except Fridays) from late May to the middle of October. The average half trip to Osier takes six to seven hours; the full trip between Chama and Antonito runs about eight hours. Return trips are made by motorcoach. You can also depart at the Cumbres Pass or Toltec Gorge.

For up-to-date information and reservations: www.cumbrestoltec.com Call 1-888-286-2737. Train stations are located in Chama, New Mexico and Antonito, Colorado.

The "Friends of the Cumbres & Toltec Scenic Railroad" also provide a fascinating 16 page list of the railroad's rolling stock at: www.cumbrestoltec.org

CHAPTER THIRTY-TWO

PENNSYLVANIA
STRASBURG RAIL ROAD ROLLS THROUGH AMISH COUNTRY
May 1986

The Strasburg Rail Road runs through Lancaster County.

Open observation car built for use in the movie "*Hello, Dolly*" starring Barbara Streisand.

STRASBURG, PENNSYLVANIA — Several hundred thousand people travel to Lancaster County annually to ride the Strasburg Rail Road through the Amish country of Pennsylvania. The forty-five minute train ride from East Strasburg to Paradise and back gives visitors a feel for what life was like a century ago.

Passengers experience this journey seated in elegant coach cars with fine wood paneling, red or green velvet seats, pot-belly stoves, and coal oil lamps. They smell the smoke from the powerful steam locomotives, hear the clacking wheels of the cars and the lonely whistle warnings at train crossings.

From their coach windows the train passengers see the Amish people living a life that may mirror their own or their parents' past. Men are plowing fields with horses or mules instead of tractors. Men and women are driving buggies pulled by horses or open farm wagons. Both the Amish and the railroad have earned important recognition in the history of Lancaster County.

The Amish were first recorded here in 1714. The railroad came to Pennsylvania in the early 1800s. According to the railroad's current website, "The Strasburg Rail Road was founded during the first term of President Andrew Jackson and incorporated by a special Act of the Pennsylvania Legislature that was signed into law by Governor George Wolf, June 9, 1832. Precisely when the railroad first turned a wheel is still a matter of patient research, but the earliest timetable found to date indicates Strasburg trains were scheduled as of December 1851." They were used for freight and passenger transportation.

The original Strasburg Rail Road fell on hard times due first to a competing electric trolley car, and some years later, the automobile. A petition for abandonment was filed with the Pennsylvania Public Utility Commission and the Interstate Commerce Commission in 1957.

However, the petition was never approved, and the railroad was rescued by a group of twenty-four enthusiastic rail fans led by Henry Long. Shares of stock were sold, and all original buyers were made vice presidents of the newly-

organized Strasburg Rail Road. The deteriorating track was 4 1/2 miles long and ran to Leaman Place.

Slowly, the railroad began to take shape. Steam engines were purchased, a parking lot built, a Victorian station moved to the East Strasburg site, a cafeteria built, gift shop concessions opened, and an old tower preserved and moved to overlook the station.

Now the Strasburg Rail Road can brag of being the oldest continuously running short line in the country.

When passengers pull out of the Strasburg Station, they will pass their first Amish farm just past Paradise Lane. Next comes a turkey farm and a crossing at Esbenshade Road (elevation 490 feet), some pine trees to the north, Cherry Hill (population 17, more or less), and Cherry Hill Road, where an Amish wagon or buggy is likely to be seen.

A picnic area called Groff's Grove follows. The last crossing is just past Carpenters Grave Yard where the engineer blows two long, one short and one long whistle before crossing Black Horse Road. An echo sounds after each blast, and the conductor tells passengers that this is the whistle of a ghost railroad.

The train then circles east, crosses a railroad bridge, runs past a forest and an old hobo camp, and arrives at Leaman Place and Paradise.

I found this historic ride fascinating, particularly because of the Amish people and their homes and farms. The railroad equipment had been beautifully restored and it was a delight to ride the train. Several types of coaches/classes were offered including: first-class parlor, deluxe lounge, dining, open air and

coach.

The modern Railroad Museum of Pennsylvania across the street owned sixty-five historic locomotives and railroad cars when I visited. They also had an extensive photo collection and thousands of railroad timetables.

In addition to the train ride, visitors to the Strasburg Rail Road can now "hop aboard a miniature steam train or use your own power by operating an authentic pump car."

For up-to-date information: www.strasburgrailroad.com Call 717-687-7522. The address is Rt. 741, East of Strasburg, Lancaster County, PA.

The Railroad Museum of Pennsylvania is located on PA Route 741, "about a mile east of the traffic signal in downtown Strasburg, which is at the intersection of Routes 896 and 741." For information: www.rrmuseumpa.org Call: 717-687-8628.

CHAPTER THIRTY-THREE

WEST VIRGINIA
CASS SCENIC RAILROAD RUNS THROUGH THE BLUE RIDGE MOUNTAINS
May 1986

A 70-ton Shay engine prepares to pull passengers up to Bald Knob, West Virginia.

CASS SCENIC RAILROAD STATE PARK, WEST VIRGINIA — Like an aged stallion puffing and snorting to impress a young filly, veteran Shay engine No. 4 rolls to a stop in front of the small depot, smoke blowing, steam hissing and whistle blowing.

It is 0900 on a weekend in early May. Members and friends of the Chesapeake and Allegheny Live Steam Society of Baltimore and Washington have traveled deep into the Blue Ridge Mountains of West Virginia to ride the famous Cass Scenic Railroad. I have flown in from Northern California just for the privilege of joining them.

The 70-ton Shay engine pulling the train was built by Lima in 1922. Locomotives 4, 5 and 7 — all West Virginia Shays — were designed for the logging operation on Cheat Mountain, a forest of red spruce trees.

At its peak, the logging operation of Cass had 1,200 men living on the mountain, twelve Shay engines in operation, and a shop in town that could repair or manufacture just about anything. A big mill with double band saws operated 24 hours-a-day putting out thousands of feet of dried lumber daily.

But by 1960, the whole operation had closed down and was fading into oblivion. When all looked

hopeless, a man from Pennsylvania with a love of trains decided to try to save the line. Russell Baum went to the West Virginia Legislature and persuaded it to buy what remained of the train equipment, tracks and shop.

Tearold Cassell, conductor on the Cass Scenic Railroad when I visited, explained, "The lumber company closed down in July '60 and the Department of Natural Resources, State of West Virginia, took it over in 1963. The first four years they just came (ran the trains) to the Whittaker Station, then in '68 started running clear up to Bald Knob. The steel track was here, but they had to replace a lot of crossties. Some 75,000 to 80,000 people come through every year. We've brought 800 up to Bald Knob in one day."

The weather was crisp and cold the day I took the ride to Bald Knob. The trees were still bare and the air filled with smoke from our engine.

The track we ran over was the standard 561/2 inches. It took us until noon to reach the top of Bald Knob, but there were stops to take on water, shoot photos, and give passengers time to take turns riding in the cab.

The trip was eleven miles and ran up from the Cass elevation of 2,452 feet to Bald Knob at 4,842 feet. We were riding in converted flatcars, now passenger coaches with gray wooden benches running the length of each car. When it got too windy, the windows could be flipped down. There was also an open observation car.

The train ran past a wooden water tower and the company shops and started a steep climb up the mountain before reaching the first switchback, an 11 percent grade. It then backed up to the second switchback before going forward again.

The locomotives labored mightily. We had slowed to a crawl while the firemen poured on more coal. Passengers could feel cinders fly against their faces and smell the black smoke as the train inched upward.

Our route took us through deeply wooded forests with a sprinkling of wildflowers just beginning to bloom. Below was Leatherbark Creek, which falls nine miles from the top of the mountain down through Leatherbark Valley.

Beyond Whittaker Station we

Cass Scenic Railroad restored caboose.

could see the ghost town of Spruce, an old logging community. Past Spruce was a ski resort called Snowshoe. We finally reached Bald Knob, the second highest spot in West Virginia. An observation deck had been built to look out over the distant valleys, but the view was hazy.

There were picnic tables on top, and we enjoyed a couple of sandwiches and a chance to stretch our legs. The locomotives panted and hissed off excess steam like live animals waiting impatiently for us to reboard. Chill mountain winds hurried our departure.

The trip back down was a repeat of the one going up except that the locomotives were located at the back.

The Cass Scenic Railroad runs daily except for Mondays from around the end of May to the beginning of September. During the fall you can ride it on weekends, and there are special schedules to take advantage of the fall colors. It is a spectacular ride.

The Mountain State Railroad & Logging Historical Association (MSR&LHA) is a non-profit group organized in 1982 which is the

"Foundation-of-Record for the Cass Scenic Railroad State Park." The park has original houses from the turn-of-the-century logging town of Cass which can be rented to visitors. In addition, you can rent a caboose or a wilderness cabin.

Cass Scenic Railroad State Park, P.O. Box 107, Cass, WV 24927. (304) 456-4300 or the West Virginia Office of Tourism, 1-800-CALL WVA.(225-5982) www.cassrailroad.com

Other special trains sound like fun:
FIDDLES AND VITTLES SPECIALS
Includes train ride to Whittaker, dinner and live bluegrass music.

MURDER MYSTERY TRAINS
Includes train ride to Whittaker, dinner and entertainment.

BIRDING AND WILDFLOWERS SPECIAL
Includes train ride and guided hikes atop Cheat Mountain. This special train is part of Cass's Whistles and Wildflower weekend and lodging packages.

HARVEST SPECIAL
A special evening train departs at 5 p.m. to Whittaker Station after a day of old-fashioned fun and games, live entertainment, costume judging and fall colors.

INDEX